INSIDE THE ANCIENT WORLD

HOMER

INSIDE THE ANCIENT WORLD

General Editor: M. R. F. Gunningham

INSIDE THE ANCIENT WORLD

HOMER

MARTIN THORPE

MACMILLAN EDUCATION

First published 1973
Reprinted 1979

Published by
MACMILLAN EDUCATION LIMITED
Houndmills Basingstoke Hampshire RG21 2XS
and London
Associated companies in Delhi Dublin
Hong Kong Johannesburg Lagos Melbourne
New York Singapore and Tokyo

Printed in Hong Kong

Contents

Acknowledgements

The author and publishers wish to acknowledge the following photograph sources.

Dept. of Antiquities, Ashmolean Museum pp.16/17
British Museum pp.27, 54, 75
German Institute, Athens p.74
Mansell Collection pp.13, 17, 52, 58, 68, 70/71, 77
Metropolitan Museum of Art, Fletcher Fund 1925 p.14
Museo Nationale di Villa Giulia, Rome p.62
National Gallery of Victoria, Melbourne p.34
Ronald Sheridan p.21
Staatlichen Antikensammlungen, Munich p.30

The publishers have made every effort to trace copyright holders, but if they have inadvertently overlooked any they will be pleased to make the necessary arrangements at the first opportunity.

List of Illustrations

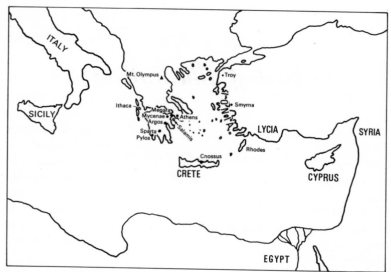

The Homeric World

General Editor's Preface

To get *inside* the Ancient World is no easy task. What is easy is to idealise the Greeks and Romans, or else unconsciously to endow them with our own conventional beliefs and prejudices. The aim of this series is to illuminate selected aspects of Antiquity in such a way as to encourage the reader to form his own judgement, from the inside, on the ways of life, culture and attitudes that characterised the Greco-Roman world. Where suitable, the books draw widely on the writings (freshly translated) of ancient authors in order to convey information and to illustrate contemporary views.

The topics in the series have been chosen both for their intrinsic interest and because of their central importance for the student who wishes to see the civilisations of Greece and Rome in perspective. The close interaction of literature, art, thought and institutions reveals the Ancient World in its totality. The opportunity should thus arise for making comparisons not only within that world, between Athens and Sparta, or Athens and Rome, but also between the world of Antiquity and our own.

The title 'Classical Studies' (or 'Classical Civilisation') is featuring more and more frequently in school timetables and in the prospectuses of universities. In schools, the subject is now examined at Advanced Level as well as at O-Level and CSE. It is particularly for the latter courses that this new series has been designed; also, as in the case of this volume, as a helpful ancillary to the study of Greek and Latin in the sixth form and below. It is hoped that some of the books will interest students of English and History at these levels as well as the non-specialist reader.

The authors, who are teachers in schools or universities, have each taken an aspect of the Ancient World. They have tried not to give a romanticised picture but to portray, as vividly as possible, the Greeks and the Romans as they really were.

Martin Thorpe's *Homer* opens with a short summary of the events of the Iliad and the Odyssey and the mythological background to the Trojan War. Subsequent chapters deal with the tradition of oral poetry in which Homer worked (The Bard); the human society of the poems, the ideal of heroic life, and the position of the lower classes (Homer and his World); the role of the gods and the attitude of mortals to them (Homer and the Gods); Homer's skill as a poet, shown both in his characterisation and in his techniques as a story-teller (Homer and the Poems); and a final chapter (Homer and History) considers the historical background to the poems and Homer's influence on the Greeks. So far as is possible, these chapters are all based upon passages from the poems – quoted, in many cases, at length.

Martin Thorpe believes that the Iliad and Odyssey are among the most approachable and enjoyable poems any student is likely to meet. His greatest fear, therefore, is that his book may come – or worse, be forced – between the student and the poems; his hope, that it may help to answer some of the many questions the poems raise in the mind of an interested reader, and may thus send him back to Homer with renewed appetite and even greater pleasure.

January 1973   MICHAEL GUNNINGHAM

I

Iliad *and* Odyssey

WHEN Peleus married the sea-nymph Thetis, the gods and goddesses came to their wedding feast. Three of the goddesses, Hera, Athena, and Aphrodite, began to argue which of them was the most beautiful. Eventually, on the advice of Zeus, they agreed to let the Trojan prince Paris decide between them. Each of the goddesses tried to bribe Paris to favour her, and Aphrodite promised that if he chose her she would give him the most beautiful of mortal women – Helen, the wife of Menelaus, king of Sparta. Paris chose Aphrodite.

Some time later Paris visited Sparta. During the absence of Menelaus Paris and Helen fell in love, fled from Sparta, and sailed off together to Troy. Attempts to recover Helen by diplomatic means failed, and Menelaus and his brother, Agamemnon, king of Mycenae, gathered a huge force of Greek warriors for an attack on Troy. Under the command of Agamemnon the expedition laid siege to Troy, but the war dragged on for ten years.

Iliad

In the tenth year of the war Chryses, a priest of Apollo, comes to the Greek camp to ask for the return of his daughter Chryseis, who has been captured on a raid and given to Agamemnon. When Agamemnon refuses to give the girl up, Chryses begs Apollo to punish the Greeks. This he does by sending a plague upon them. A few days later Achilles, the greatest of the Greek warriors, calls an assembly of the Greek forces to discover how they can bring the plague to an end. The prophet Calchas explains why Apollo is angry with the Greeks and proposes that Agamemnon should give up Chryseis. Agamemnon reluctantly agrees but insists that the other Greek leaders must make good his loss by providing him with another girl. When Achilles protests, Agamemnon sends men to take away Briseis, a captive girl who had been assigned to Achilles.

Achilles is furious at this insult. He refuses to take any further part in

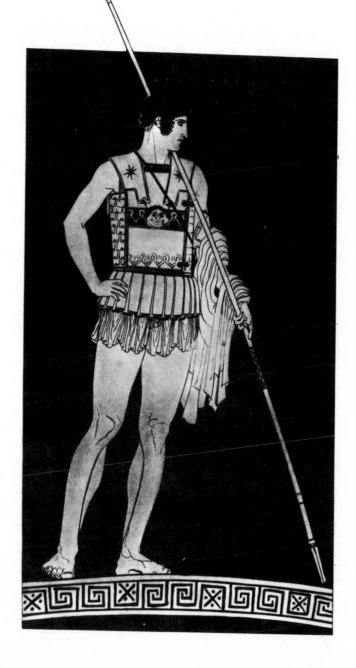

1. *Achilles, the ideal hero: 'always to be best and excel other men'.* [*Iliad* XI 784]

the fighting and asks his mother Thetis to persuade Zeus to humble Agamemnon and the Greeks. Zeus agrees to this request (Book I).

On the next day Agamemnon marshals the Greek forces for an attack on the Trojans. In general, the Greeks have the better of the day's fighting, and Diomedes in particular carries all before him (Books II–VII).

On the second day of battle Zeus' plan to avenge Achilles begins to take effect and the Greeks are driven back. At the end of the day the Trojans do not return to their city but camp out confidently on the plain ready for an onslaught on the Greek camp next day. Agamemnon now realises how greatly his army depends upon Achilles and he sends an embassy to him admitting that he was wrong and offering to restore Briseis and give Achilles many other gifts if he will rejoin the fighting. Achilles refuses. To keep up morale Odysseus and Diomedes make a night attack upon the camp of one of the Trojan allies (Books VIII–X).

After an encouraging start to the third day's fighting the Greeks are again driven back and all their greatest heroes except Ajax are wounded and forced to leave the battle. The Trojans burst through the Greek defences and are on the point of setting fire to their ships. At this stage Patroclus approaches his friend Achilles and begs leave to borrow his armour and to lead his men to the rescue. These reinforcements turn the tide, and the Greeks move on to the attack once more, until the Trojan leader Hector kills Patroclus. Hector strips Achilles' armour from Patroclus but after a great struggle the Greeks manage to save his body and bring it back to their camp. Despite this they are soon in full retreat again. When Achilles hears of his friend's death he comes to the ditch which surrounds the Greek camp and shouts his battle-cry. This terrifies the Trojans and allows the Greeks to return in safety to their camp (Books X–XVIII).

By now Achilles' anger against Agamemnon has subsided, driven out by the hatred he now feels for Hector. His mother Thetis has a new suit of armour made for him by the divine blacksmith, Hephaestus. Next morning Achilles calls an assembly and announces the end of his quarrel with Agamemnon and his decision to re-enter the fighting. He sweeps the Trojans from the plain and forces them to retire inside the walls of their city. Hector and Achilles meet outside Troy. At first Hector tries to escape, but when he sees this is impossible he turns and stands his ground. Achilles kills him, attaches his body to the back of his chariot, and drags him back to the Greek camp (Books XVIII–XXII).

The next day Achilles celebrates the funeral of Patroclus. He burns his body on a pyre and then holds games – athletic events – in his honour. He continues to insult the body of Hector by dragging it daily round the walls of Troy. After twelve days king Priam of Troy, the father of Hector, ventures by night into the Greek camp and offers a great ransom to

2. *Hector dragged behind the chariot of Achilles.*

Achilles for the body of his son. Achilles allows Priam to take it, and ten days later the Trojans celebrate Hector's funeral (Books XXIII and XXIV).

On the day after Hector's funeral fighting began again between the Greeks and the Trojans. After further successes Achilles himself was killed, wounded in the heel by an arrow from the archer Paris. Eventually, the craftiest of the Greeks, Odysseus, suggested the stratagem of the Wooden Horse. By this means the Greeks gained admittance to Troy. They soon overcame all resistance. Achilles' son Neoptolemus killed King Priam, the city was plundered, and the Trojan women were assigned as prizes of war to the various Greek leaders. The Greeks set fire to Troy and began the voyage back to their own land.

Several of the Greek leaders met with trouble either at sea or when they reached home. Their adventures were also recounted in verse. The most famous of these stories, apart from the *Odyssey* itself, was that of Agamemnon, who was murdered on his return by his faithless wife Clytaemnestra and her lover Aegisthus.

Ten years after the end of the Trojan War Odysseus had still not returned to his home on Ithaca. During his absence a large group of nobles from the surrounding areas had come to his palace in the hope of persuading Odysseus' wife Penelope to marry again. Though she refused to accept any one of them, they remained on the island enjoying themselves in the palace at Odysseus' expense.

In the tenth year the crisis in Ithaca came to a head. Penelope could not put off the choice of a new husband much longer, and Odysseus' son Telemachus, a mere baby when his father left for Troy, had grown up and was anxious to assert his rights by driving the suitors out of the palace.

Odyssey

In a council of the gods Athena persuades Zeus that it is now time to allow Odysseus to return home. She then visits Ithaca in disguise and advises Telemachus to go to Pylos and Sparta in the hope of finding out whether his father is still alive and where he is. Telemachus agrees. King Nestor of Pylos and Menelaus, now happily settled again with Helen at Sparta, entertain Telemachus generously. They praise his father's great exploits at Troy but have no definite news of him (Books I–IV).

Meanwhile Odysseus has been spending the last seven years on an island with the nymph Calypso. He knows that she loves him and would like to make him immortal but he still longs to leave her and return home to Penelope. After the council of the gods, Hermes visits Calypso and brings her Zeus' instructions: she must release Odysseus. Odysseus is delighted, builds a raft and sets sail for Ithaca. When he has been at sea for seventeen days and is making good progress towards Ithaca, Poseidon notices the raft and rouses a storm to destroy it. Odysseus is wrecked off the coast of Scheria, but the inhabitants of that island, the Phaeacians, and their king, Alcinous, receive him kindly. At first Odysseus does not reveal his identity, but as he listens to the Phaeacian court poet tell the story of the Wooden Horse he breaks down and admits that he is Odysseus. The Phaeacians insist on hearing the story of his adventures (Books V–VIII).

In the next four books Odysseus describes what happened to him on the way home from Troy before he came to Calypso's island. This section of the poem contains many of the most famous stories about Odysseus, including his encounters with the Cyclops (Book IX) and with Circe (Book X), his visit to the Underworld (Book XI), and his dangerous voyage past the Sirens and between Scylla and Charybdis (Book XII).

The next night the Phaeacians take Odysseus home to Ithaca. Disguised as a beggar, he makes his way to the hut of one of his slaves, Eumaeùs, and finds out about the situation in his palace. When Telemachus

4. *Odysseus and the Sirens.*

3. *Odysseus and Circe:*
'*Circe mixed a drink for
me in a golden cup and put
a drug in it. When she
gave it to me, I drank it
down but was not
bewitched. Then Circe
struck me with her wand
and said: "Now go off to
the sty and bed down with
the rest of your friends."
But I drew my sharp
sword and sprang at
Circe as though I
intended to kill her.*'
[*Odyssey* x 316–22]

returns from Sparta he too makes first for Eumaeus' hut, and on the next day, while Eumaeus is out at work, Odysseus reveals who he is to his son (Books XIII–XVI).

The scene now switches to Odysseus' palace. Disguised again as a beggar Odysseus enters the hall where the suitors are feasting. They ridicule and insult him, but Odysseus bears this patiently. Inspired by the goddess Athena, Penelope now sets a test for the suitors: she brings out Odysseus' great bow and announces that she will marry whichever of the suitors can string it and shoot an arrow through a line of axe-heads set in the floor of the palace. All the suitors make the attempt, but all fail even to string it. The beggar now asks permission to try, and despite objections from the suitors the bow is brought to him. He examines it in silence for a few moments, turning it over in his hands, then strings it easily and shoots an arrow straight through the line of axe-heads (Books XVII–XXI).

The need for disguise is over; Odysseus strips off his rags, takes up a position by the door, and begins to shoot down the suitors. Before long the slaughter is complete. Odysseus makes himself known to Penelope, and the palace is cleaned and purified. Odysseus then visits his father Laertes, who is living in misery and squalor on his farm outside the town. Meanwhile the relatives of the murdered suitors gather to attack Odysseus, but just as the battle begins the gods intervene and peace is made between the two groups (Books XXII–XXIV).

2

The Bard

Demodocus

THE morning after Odysseus' arrival in Scheria King Alcinous calls a meeting of the Phaeacian nobles. He suggests that they make ready a ship and crew to take Odysseus back home and then invites the chief nobles to join him in entertaining Odysseus in his palace; in particular, he gives orders that the Phaeacian bard, Demodocus, be summoned.

After they have entered the palace, a herald leads in Demodocus:

> the Muse loved him above all others but she had given him both good and evil gifts; she had made him blind but had endowed him with the gift of sweet song. [*Odyssey* VIII 63–4.]

He is placed on a chair in the midst of the company and given his lyre, and a table with food and wine is placed beside him.

> The Muse inspired the bard to sing of the exploits of heroes, choosing a passage from a well-known tale, the story of the quarrel between Odysseus and Achilles. [*Odyssey* VIII 73–5.]

When he hears this Odysseus is overcome with emotion; and though he manages to hide his grief from the other Phaeacians, Alcinous notices his tears. Immediately he intervenes to suggest that, as they have all feasted enough, they should go outside. Demodocus is thus forced to break off his song.

Outside, the young noblemen compete in various athletic events – footrace, wrestling, jumping, discus – and then invite Odysseus to join them. When he refuses, one of them insults him. Stung into action Odysseus hurls a huge stone further than any of the Phaeacians and angrily issues a general challenge. Again Alcinous intervenes to smoothe things over, pointing out that the Phaeacians are not particularly good at athletics but that dancing and music are among their chief pleasures. He calls forward a team of champion dancers and sends someone to fetch Demodocus' lyre from the palace. Once given his lyre, Demodocus

> went out into the middle of the dancing area, and young men who were expert dancers took up their positions around him and beat out a rapid dance with their feet. Odysseus admired its scintillating

movement. Presently the bard began a beautiful song. . . . [*Odyssey* VIII 262–6.]

On this occasion, though, Demodocus does not take an incident from the Trojan War but in keeping with the needs of the moment and the glittering pattern of the dance tells a sophisticated story of the love of Ares and Aphrodite – indeed, it is perhaps the earliest short story in European literature.

At sunset the company returns to the palace for more feasting, and Demodocus is brought in again. Odysseus sends him some food, observing that

> 'Bards enjoy honour and respect from all men, for the Muse teaches them their songs and loves them all.' [*Odyssey* VIII 479–81.]

At the end of the meal Odysseus turns to Demodocus and asks him to tell the story of the Wooden Horse:

> 'Demodocus, I admire you more than anyone in the world, for either the Muse, the daughter of Zeus, has taught you or else Apollo. . . . If you tell this story correctly, I shall tell everyone how generously the god has given you the divine gift of song.' That was what Odysseus said and the bard, filled with divine inspiration, unfolded the tale, beginning at the point where the Greeks had set fire to their huts and were sailing off. [*Odyssey* VIII 487–502.]

However, before Demodocus has got far into his story, Odysseus breaks down again and Alcinous orders him to stop.

Phemius

We meet another of these bards in Ithaca itself. In *Odyssey* I, Phemius, the court poet of Odysseus' kingdom, is entertaining Penelope's suitors with the story of the return of the Greek heroes from Troy. Penelope rebukes him for choosing this story when he knows so many others, but Telemachus defends him:

> 'You shouldn't blame Phemius for singing of the unhappy fate of the Greeks, for the latest story always wins most applause from the audience.' [*Odyssey* I 350–2.]

Later in the poem, when Odysseus has massacred the suitors, Phemius comes forward to beg for mercy, insisting that he only sang for the suitors because he was compelled to do so.

> 'I beg you to have pity on me, Odysseus, and show some respect for my position. If you kill a bard who sings for men and gods, you will have grief hereafter. I am self-taught, a god has inspired me

with the power to sing all kinds of songs. I am fit to sing before you as before a god. Don't cut my throat.' [*Odyssey* XXII 344–9.]

Odysseus spares him.

Oral poetry

The details Homer gives us of the life and work of these two men demonstrate the important role such bards and their narrative poems, or songs, had in Homeric society. They claim, and receive, considerable respect and clearly regard themselves as – in the modern phrase – 'creative artists'. (The stress they lay upon divine inspiration is intended to emphasise this fact, not to minimise it, and one should interpret Phemius' claim to be self-taught in the same way: their poetry comes from within themselves.)

5. *Greek Bard, eighth century* B.C.

6. *Yugoslav Bard, twentieth century* A.D.

Yet they are very unlike our modern picture of a poet. Demodocus holds a respected position in Phaeacian society but it is still a subordinate one; he is not independent but a member of the king's household, a kind of superior servant. He has a large repertoire of songs from which to choose but cannot always make the choice himself; for example, he is obliged to accept Odysseus' suggestion that he sing about the Wooden Horse. He cannot even choose when he will sing and when remain silent, for he is clearly expected to be ready with a poem to suit every occasion. In some ways, therefore, he seems more of a performer than a creative artist.

In fact, of course, he is both. These are illiterate poets working in a long tradition of oral poetry and relying upon its special techniques to compose as they perform. Homer himself belongs to this tradition, and it is part of the importance of these portraits of Demodocus and Phemius that they give us some idea of the way Homer may have worked.

Oral poetry is not something found only in ancient Greece, but is known from many countries and many ages. Narrative poems composed within an oral tradition were a feature of Anglo-Saxon England (the best known poem which derives from this tradition is *Beowulf*), and our knowledge of Norse mythology, for instance, comes ultimately from a similar source. The tribes of central Asia, the Maoris of New Zealand, and the American Indians are some of the other peoples who produced and enjoyed oral poetry. In some parts of the world the tradition still survives and the oral poetry of Yugoslavia in particular has been studied in great detail in this century. It has been possible to record the narrative poems, sung by illiterate bards, and to question their authors closely about their composition and performance; a comparison of poems and answers has greatly increased our knowledge of oral poetry.

In the remainder of this chapter we shall look at certain features of this tradition as it appears in the *Iliad* and *Odyssey* to try to build up a picture of how an oral poet, and hence Homer, was able to compose a long poem in performance. This may also help to explain certain features of the poem which sometimes puzzle the reader.

Formulae

Every reader of the *Iliad* and *Odyssey* is struck by the frequent recurrence of such phrases as 'Diomedes of the loud war-cry', 'Agamemnon, King of Men', 'bright-eyed Athena', and 'Achilles of the nimble feet'. It is fairly easy to appreciate the general sheen of heroic splendour these phrases cast upon the poems as a whole, but important also to realise that the true reason for their use is more down-to-earth and less 'poetic'.

An oral poet composes not with single words but with phrases, units already created in the correct metre for his poem. These phrases, or formulae, and not the words of which they are made up, are the bricks from which the architecture of the poems is constructed. Thus, when writing of Diomedes, Homer does not choose by the addition of the words 'of the loud war-cry' to remind his audience of a specific feature of Diomedes' excellence as a warrior. Under certain linguistic and rhythmical conditions this is the only way in which he can refer to him.

This type of formula, in which the name of a hero or god is qualified by some descriptive word or phrase, is probably the most obvious to an English reader, but it is certainly not the only one. Similar phrases are available for things too – 'long-shadowing spear', 'curved ships', for example – and there are also formulae for most of the commonly recurring actions of the poems:

So all day long, until the sun set, we sat feasting on abundant meat and sweet wine, but when the sun set and darkness came on, then . . . .

or 'He fell with a thud, and his armour clanged about him'.

The poet has a personal vocabulary of formulae adequate for any story which he may decide or be called upon to sing. Part of it will be traditional, consisting of formulae handed down by word of mouth from older singers and the common property of all poets living in a particular area at any one time. Another part will be more recent, including some phrases which he may have taken over from his contemporaries and others of his own creation, alterations to or adaptations of the traditional patterns. In turn, some of these may come to be considered traditional by succeeding generations of bards. The tradition is not rigid, but constantly changing. Each poet unconsciously absorbs what he requires from it and ignores the rest. It is a support to the singer, not a strait-jacket.

Themes

The existence of such formulae, phrases which not only convey information but do so in a metrically convenient form, is one of the features of the oral tradition which makes it possible for the bard to compose as he performs. The poet also works with larger units, usually called themes, which may be described as the different narrative or descriptive elements which go to make up a complete poem. Such incidents as the arming of a hero, the mustering of an army for battle, a council of the gods, or the beaching of a ship at nightfall, with the disembarkation of the sailors, their preparations for supper, sleep on the seashore and departure the next day are likely to recur frequently in heroic poetry, and a competent bard will have a clear idea of how he will wish to handle them.

On an even larger scale one could class as themes such matters as a quarrel between two heroes or the return of a hero from the wars and the difficulties he finds when he reaches home. Whether the quarrel is the one between Achilles and Agamemnon which forms the starting point of the *Iliad* or takes place between Odysseus and Achilles, as in the poem which Demodocus began to sing, many of the incidents which the bard uses in his description of it will be the same. Certain of the adventures which Homer makes Odysseus undergo in the *Odyssey* seem also to have been associated with the voyage of Jason and the Argonauts in search of the Golden Fleece.

Composition and performance

We can see how a wide repertory of themes helps a singer by considering the evidence from Yugoslavia. An illiterate bard was asked whether, if he heard another bard sing a song, he could repeat it. His answer was confident: 'It's possible. . . . I know from my own experience. When I was together with my brothers and had nothing to worry about, I would hear a singer sing a song . . . and after an hour I would sing his whole song. I can't write. I would give every word and not make a mistake on a single one.' He admitted, though, that if two singers listened to a third and then sang the song they had heard, there would inevitably be differences. Further questioning made it clear that what these bards meant by 'learning a song' was discovering what themes went to make up its story-line. Once they knew that, they could repeat it, using of course the same themes in the same order but telling them in their own personal way. Similarly, singers boasted that if they were to repeat a song in ten years it would be precisely the same song 'word for word', but experience showed that their claim was false and that though it remained recognisably the same story there was always some change in its wording.

An oral poet who possesses a wide vocabulary of formulae and a good stock of themes can create a poem in performance. Two further features of this 'composition in performance' require comment. Firstly, since the poem is composed as it is performed, it is impossible for the poet to go back to correct any mistakes he may have made or to improve the early part of the poem. Once he has started he must go on. It is therefore wrong to expect from an oral poet the sort of consistency of detail we take for granted in the work of a poet or novelist nowadays. The oral poet is forced to concentrate all his attention on the incident which he is actually singing at each moment.

Secondly, and more importantly, he does not compose in private, locked in his study, but in public, and the attitude of his audience will have a significant effect on his performance. To start with, the audience may tell him what song to sing, as Odysseus asked Demodocus to sing about the Wooden Horse. Even when he has started, he can never feel that he is free to compose as he would like, for he cannot tell how long he will be allowed to continue and hence on what scale to create his poem – whether to draw it out and enrich it with additional detail or whether to keep it brief, a mere summary of the main incidents in the story. If he decides to expand, he may find that his audience begins to get restless, to start talking, or to show more interest in the wine than in his poem, and he will then be obliged to speed up his narrative, packing in more action in a desperate attempt to reawaken their flagging interest. If fear of this possibility makes him choose the second way, he may find that his poem is too brief and insubstantial – too lacking in motivation, for instance – to please the audience. And, in either case, new arrivals, a drunken quarrel, or a sudden change of plan may stop him in his tracks. No two performances of a song can ever be quite the same.

Iliad and Odyssey

When we return to the *Iliad* and *Odyssey*, two problems at once confront us – the great length of the poems and the question of how and when they were written down. The problems are interconnected, for both involve a new attitude to traditional narrative poetry. We do not know how long Demodocus' poem about the Wooden Horse would have been, but it was clearly intended that it would be complete that night; the *Iliad* and *Odyssey* would each have taken, at a rough estimate, between fifty and sixty hours to recite.

For what audience, on what occasion were the poems composed? Who could have commissioned them? To go further, who would have broken with tradition by deciding that the poems should be written down, that for once a particular performance should not be forgotten when it ended but should be accurately recorded?

Various solutions have been suggested. Some scholars have thought that a major religious festival lasting several days might have provided an ideal opportunity for a bard to compose at greater length than usual. Some have suggested that Homer dictated the poems to scribes. Others believe that this would have been extraordinarily cumbersome; they prefer to think that Homer's poems must first have been learned by heart from his lips, then remembered accurately for several generations, and only later written down. At the moment these problems remain unsolved.

7. *Greek Singer, reciting an epic poem, from a vase painting of about 480* B.C.

What we can say is that the composition of the *Iliad* and *Odyssey* probably occurred at some time during the second half of the eighth century BC, for they contain references to objects and practices which cannot be dated before about 750. But the tradition to which they belong must have originated at least four hundred years earlier, for knowledge of the Mycenaean objects mentioned in the poems could only have survived through the medium of the tradition. (For the relations between Homer, the poems, and history see Chapter 6.)

3
Homer and his World

Heroes

WE have seen what it means to describe the *Iliad* and *Odyssey* as oral epics. Another name sometimes used for this type of poetry is 'heroic epic'. This is because it deals mainly with the exploits and achievements of heroes and because such heroes – the word itself is Greek – as Achilles and Agamemnon often act and think in much the same way as the characters of oral epic from other lands and ages.

This can be summed up most clearly in the advice which Achilles was given by his father Peleus: 'always to be best and excel other men' [*Iliad* XI 784]. The hero's attitude is competitive; it is not enough merely to do well, he must do better than other men. His aim is to win honour and respect in his lifetime and to leave behind him a name which will continue to be celebrated, in heroic epic, by later generations.

Success in almost any field can increase a man's status. Even lying and deception, if good enough, win some respect. When Odysseus returns to Ithaca he meets the goddess Athena disguised as a shepherd and, instead of telling the truth, he spins a story that he was a Cretan who had left the island after murdering a man. Athena is delighted by his cunning and describes him as 'far surpassing all men in deceit and clever speaking' [*Odyssey* XIII 297]. In another of the lies he tells to deceive the people in Ithaca Odysseus claims that he was a Cretan pirate:

> I always liked seafaring and warfare – dreadful things that other people hate. I suppose that's how god made me, for different people take to different ways of life. . . . I gained a great deal of plunder. . . . My household flourished and I became a powerful and respected figure among the Cretans. [*Odyssey* XIV 225–34.]

Athletics

Athletic competitions provide obvious opportunities for men to match themselves against their rivals, to show their skill, and to enjoy the glory that comes from victory and the applause of the crowd. We have already

8. *Chariot Race.*

seen how Odysseus was forced to compete in the games held by the
Phaeacians, but a better example of how intensely the heroes felt the
pressure to win, and to be seen to win, occurs in the chariot race which
forms part of the funeral games which Achilles puts on in honour of
Patroclus.

Towards the end of the race Menelaus was slightly in front of
Antilochus. Ahead of them was a place where the road narrowed and
passed through a deep gulley. Noticing this and urging his horses on,
Antilochus drew almost level with Menelaus and refused to drop back as
they approached the defile. It was Menelaus who

> eased the pace, for he was afraid that the horses would collide and
> overturn the chariots and that, through their eagerness to win, he
> and Antilochus would be flung out into the dust. [*Iliad* XXIII
> 434–7.]

Antilochus came in ahead of Menelaus and was just about to receive his
prize when Menelaus entered an angry protest against his unfair tactics:

'Antilochus, you have behaved disgracefully; you have damaged my reputation as a charioteer and injured my horses by thrusting your horses in front of mine though they are far less good.' [*Iliad* XXIII 570–2.]

Antilochus accepts the point and surrenders the prize to Menelaus.

War

But it is, of course, in war that the competitive spirit of the heroic age finds its clearest and most typical expression. The hero must always be prepared to stake his reputation in the hope of increasing it, and the greatest honour comes where the risks are greatest and the penalty for failure most final.

Since success in battle is so important it is not surprising that we find more evidence for the heroic temperament in the *Iliad* than in the *Odyssey*. The greatest warrior of the Trojan War was, without doubt, Achilles, but the very fact that he is the central figure of the *Iliad* makes him a rather untypical figure and it is probably better to use two of the lesser, though still front-rank, heroes to illustrate the heroic spirit.

Diomedes

Like most of the Greek heroes, Diomedes is introduced into the poem in the so-called 'Catalogue of the Greeks' in *Iliad* II (559–68). He rules over the city of Argos and its surrounding area and the contingent of eighty ships which he leads is one of the largest in the Greek force. His character is clearly established early in the first day's fighting when he remains silent under some rather unfair criticism from Agamemnon and reproaches his lieutenant Sthenelus for answering back. He recognises that like any other hero Agememnon is motivated by a desire for glory. Indeed, this whole-hearted acceptance of the heroic way of life is just what characterises Diomedes; young, vigorous, successful, he revels in battle in a spirit almost of play. The absence of Achilles allows him to shine, and in the fighting described in *Iliad* V and VI he sweeps all before him. He is supported by Athena, who makes his shield and helmet blaze with a brilliant light, and with her encouragement he even dares to attack three of the Olympian gods. One incident in particular is worth recounting in detail.

In the course of the battle Diomedes comes face to face with a young warrior on the Trojan side whom he does not recognise. He enquires who he is. The other replies that his name is Glaucus and that he has recently come from Lycia to join the Trojan forces; his family, though, is Greek and he is descended from Bellerophon who came from the city of Corinth not far from Diomedes' own city Argos.

> Diomedes was delighted when he heard this. He drove his spear into the ground and spoke warmly to Glaucus. 'See now, you and I are friends – there is a tie of hospitality dating far back to our grandfathers' time. . . . So I am your friend and host in Argos, you mine in Lycia if ever I come to your country. Let us keep clear of each other's spears in the fighting. There are plenty of Trojans and their allies for me to kill . . . and plenty of Greeks for you. And let us exchange armour so that people will recognise that we are friends from long ago and proud to own it.' With these words they leapt down from their chariots and clasped each other's hands and swore to be friends. Then Zeus robbed Glaucus of his wits, for in return for Diomedes' bronze armour he gave him his golden armour, exchanging what was worth a hundred oxen for what was worth only nine. [*Iliad* VI 212–36.]

The whole scene of Diomedes' success in these books has a brilliant quality which shows the heroic world in a most attractive light. Despite the bloodshed there is a lightness and confidence here that is quite different from the superficially similar but far more sombre nature of the scenes of Achilles' battle successes in *Iliad* XIX–XXII.

In the fighting on the next day the battle swings in favour of the Trojans. As the Greeks fall back, the old man Nestor is cut off and appeals for assistance first to Odysseus, who ignores him, then to Diomedes. He immediately goes up to Nestor and takes him into his own chariot. Together they move into the attack as Diomedes makes for Hector, but Zeus halts him:

> He thundered terribly and sent a flash of lightning to the ground just in front of Diomedes' horses. There was a flash and a smell of burning sulphur and the horses reared back in fear. [*Iliad* VIII 133–6.]

Nestor advises retreat, and reluctantly Diomedes agrees, though it involves him in terrible risk to his reputation.

> 'Your advice is good, old man, but brings great grief to my heart. For Hector will say to the Trojans "Diomedes was terrified of me and went back to the ships". That's what he will claim.' [*Iliad* VIII 146–50.]

With all we know of Diomedes' character, we are not in the least surprised to learn that that evening he is the first to volunteer when Nestor suggests that a night raid on the Trojan camp would be of help to the Greeks.

In *Iliad* XI Diomedes is wounded by an arrow from Paris' bow and is forced to leave the battle, and in the remainder of the poem he is far less prominent. From this point on until Patroclus enters the battle dressed in Achilles' armour and again from his death until Achilles' eventual intervention the Greek are hard pressed to defend their ships. In these defensive operations Diomedes' attacking spirit would hardly be appropriate, and his place as the most effective warrior on the Greek side is taken by the less brilliant but weightier Ajax, whom the Greek tradition called the greatest of the Greek warriors after Achilles. Moreover, once Achilles has entered the battle and the Greeks resume the offensive, there can still be no place for Diomedes. He is an admirable substitute for the spirit of attack in the Greek forces while Achilles kept to his tent, but he is too bright a figure, too uncomplicated, ultimately perhaps too trivial, for the tragic and complex situation in which the Greeks are now involved.

We have only one more picture of Diomedes in the *Iliad*, and it is a typical one. In the funeral games in honour of Patroclus he takes part in a duel with Ajax and is the victor in the chariot race.

Sarpedon

Sarpedon, leader of the troops from Lycia and cousin of Glaucus, is one of the most prominent of the allies who have come to the support of the Trojans. During the Greek success in the first day's fighting he bitterly rebukes Hector for hanging back and urges the Trojans to counter-attack. In the fighting that follows he meets the Greek hero Tlepolemus, son of Heracles, who opens the encounter with an aggressive, insulting speech and boasts that he will soon kill Sarpedon. Sarpedon's speech is restrained; he admits Heracles' great achievements but is confident that he will kill Tlepolemus. Tlepolemus is killed, Sarpedon wounded.

He recovers, however, and his greatest moment comes in the third day's fighting, when he is the first to break down the rampart the Greeks have built around their camp. As they advance to the attack, Sarpedon speaks to Glaucus:

'Glaucus, why are we two honoured more than other men in Lycia, with the best seats at the feast and meat and full cups of wine? Why do all men look up to us as gods? And we have been given a great estate of orchard and plough-land beside the river Xanthus. Because of these honours we must always be in the forefront of the Lycians in the heat of battle; then the Lycians will say "Our kings who rule over Lycia enjoy the choicest meat and wine, but they are indeed glorious and mighty, for they fight in the forefront of the Lycians." My friend, if a safe escape from this war meant that we should be for ever ageless and immortal, I should not fight in the front line myself nor

9. *Greeks and Trojans fighting, as seen by a vase painter of the sixth century* B.C.

urge you into the battle where men win glory. But, as it is, death stands in wait in a thousand forms, no mortal can escape it. Let us go forward then – and either bring glory on some other man or win it ourselves.' [*Iliad* XII 310–28.]

Later that day, when a complete Trojan victory seems assured, the Greeks rally around Patroclus, dressed in the armour of Achilles. As the Trojans are driven back Patroclus kills Sarpedon. Their combat and the subsequent fight over Sarpedon's body make up one of the richest and most sublime pieces of battle narrative in the *Iliad*. [XVI 419–683.]

The heroic spirit

These passages throw a rich light on the heroic spirit. They reveal how the hero looks at the world and his ideas about his place in it. The hero knows that he is bound to die. This fact is fundamental for him; he lives with it all the time, and it shapes his whole experience of life. His life is always in danger – 'death stands in wait in a thousand forms' – and indeed a man cannot become a hero unless he is prepared to risk his life.

Moreover the hero could not comfort himself for the dangers of this life by concentrating on a life after death. The Homeric world did have some belief in an after-life, but the sort of existence described in *Odyssey* XI (Odysseus' visit to Hades) was too shadowy and insubstantial to have much appeal.

We also know that we will die, but this fact does not seem so important to us. In the normal course of events we expect to live out our normal span of years, we make long-term plans for the future, and are surprised and shocked when we hear of someone dying young. Our life seems much more secure than the hero's.

Knowing that his life might end at any time, the hero tried to create something permanent and lasting by winning glory. He wanted men to honour him in his lifetime and remember his achievements even after his death. If other people did not notice what he did, all his effort would have been in vain; public recognition was essential. The Lycians publicly honoured Sarpedon and Glaucus by giving them 'the best seats at the feast and meat and full cups of wine'. When a hero received such honour, he felt obliged – as Sarpedon did – to respect the opinion men had of him and to try to live up to it.

Single combat

At the start of the 'Catalogue' in *Iliad* II Homer compares the size of the Greek forces to the huge flocks of birds that gather in the meadows beside the river Kayster in Ionia and to the swarms of insects which cloud around the sheep-pens in summer. He adds an appeal to the Muses:

> Even if I had ten tongues and ten mouths, a voice that never tired and a heart of bronze I could not name the great mass of them, unless you prompted my memory, Muses. [*Iliad* II 488–92.]

It may seem rather strange, therefore, that once the fighting begins, Homer seems to forget almost entirely about these masses and instead presents the war as a succession of single combats between individual heroes. This is not just a useful narrative technique: it has the further advantage of making us concentrate on the behaviour of these heroes at moments of crisis. We can see Antilochus kill Echepolus or Tlepolemus fall to Sarpedon. Homer thus gives us the evidence we need to make up our own minds about their status as heroes.

These combats frequently begin with the heroes exchanging names and boasting to each other of their great achievements. This habit can easily seem arrogant and aggressive but can also, as in the meeting between Diomedes and Glaucus or in Sarpedon's reply to Tlepolemus, be restrained and courteous. One motive for it – the need to publicise one's own achievements – we have already seen. Once the custom is established, though, another motive may also operate. The demands of heroic competition are harsh, for the hero can only assert his claims by destroying others', but such practices add a touch of dignity and formality to the struggle – they are, as it were, the rules of the game – and so help to make it tolerable.

The speeches the heroes deliver on these occasions also show the vast importance the Greeks attached to genealogies and to the details of family history. The delight of Diomedes when he hears Glaucus' history demonstrates that friendship between families could still be effective two generations after it was first formed.

After the boasts comes the actual fighting, leading to the wounding or death of one of the combatants. The death of a major hero is often followed by another struggle over his corpse. If the victor can drag the body of his defeated rival back to the safety of his own lines and there rob it of its armour, he has in his possession visible proof of his success in battle.

Heroic society was highly competitive

The highly competitive nature of heroic society has been stressed in this chapter, and evidence of it could be found throughout the *Iliad* and *Odyssey*. It is a slight to Achilles' honour which leads to his quarrel with Agamemnon and so sets the action of the *Iliad* in motion; the story of

Meleager, which Phoenix tells in an attempt to persuade Achilles to return to battle [*Iliad* IX 434–605], provides a parallel situation; Demodocus starts to sing about the 'well-known' quarrel of Achilles and Odysseus (see Chapter 2); later tradition tells us that Odysseus and Ajax quarrelled over the armour of Achilles; even the trivial dispute between Idomeneus and Ajax as to which of the competitors in the chariot race is in the lead – the figures are still too far distant to be clearly distinguished – begins to look distinctly ugly until Achilles intervenes [*Iliad* XXIII 450–98]. And it is because the heroes are so touchy and so unwilling to submerge their own claims to respect in the general interest of the whole Greek force that the position of Agamemnon as commander-in-chief is so difficult. He can impose his decisions – as in ordering Achilles to surrender Briseis in *Iliad* I – but they are not always accepted with a good grace.

One can also point to the many cases where a hero is forced to leave his own country. Glaucus tells Diomedes how Bellerophon was obliged to leave Corinth; Phoenix, in the speech mentioned above, reminds Achilles how he fled to the court of Achilles' father, Peleus, after a quarrel with his own father; in the lying story Odysseus tells Athena on his return to Ithaca he pretends that he had been compelled to leave Crete after he had murdered a man.

What kept it together?

It might seem, then, that a society in which the forces of division were so strong would collapse into anarchy, and it is worth enquiring what counter-forces there were which could help to keep it together.

(a) Kinship

One of the most obvious is kinship. As one would expect, members of the same family or clan usually co-operated. It is true that quarrels could occur, as the cases of Bellerophon and Phoenix show, and then the very closeness of the family would make them particularly intense, so that exile might well be the only possible solution. These, however, are the exceptions, and examples of family co-operation are easy to find. One of the reasons for Agamemnon's command in the war against Troy is that he is Menelaus' brother; family ties involve him directly in the struggle for the return of Helen. Again, throughout the *Odyssey* there runs a comparison between the families of Agamemnon and Odysseus. On his return from Troy, Agamemnon was murdered by his wife Clytaemnestra and her lover Aegisthus: Penelope remains a model of fidelity to Odysseus however long his wanderings. Agamemnon's son Orestes avenged his father by

killing Clytaemnestra and Aegisthus: Odysseus' son Telemachus is urged
to follow his example of family loyalty.

(b) Guest-friendship and Guest-gifts

The institution of guest-friendship links separate families. In an age
without hotels or inns a traveller is obliged to rely for food and lodg-
ing on the hospitality of others, and it was a strictly observed custom
of the Greek heroic world that the peaceful traveller should receive this
hospitality wherever he went. The bond between host and guest was
considered of supreme importance. It was a most serious crime for either
to take advantage of the situation by injuring or defrauding the other;
indeed, without some such custom travel outside a man's home area
would have been almost impossible. It is not surprising, therefore, that
one of the particular tasks assigned to Zeus is the protection of strangers.

Once the link between host and guest was made it became hereditary
and was usually formalised by an exchange of gifts. This was not just a
pleasant gesture: the gifts were intended to demonstrate publicly the
alliance thus created between the two men, and the value of the gift a
man received showed what other people thought of him and so helped to
fix his status in society. The whole practice is clearly illustrated by the
passage we have already mentioned so often, the description of the meeting
between Diomedes and Glaucus. When Diomedes hears of Glaucus'
ancestry he recognises an already existing link between them and wishes
to renew it and 'republish' it by a second exchange of gifts. The incident
ends, though, in absurdity, for though the heroes meet and talk as equals,
the exchange of armour contradicts this equality, for

> Zeus robbed Glaucus of his wits, for in return for Diomedes' bronze
> armour he gave him his golden armour, exchanging what was worth
> a hundred oxen for what was worth only nine. [*Iliad* VI 234–6.]

Many other passages from the *Iliad* and *Odyssey* illustrate the importance
of guest-friendship and guest-gifts. At the briefest, there is the description
of Telemachus' stop at Pherae at the end of the second day of his journey
to Sparta: 'There they spent the night, and Diocles gave them guest-gifts'
[*Odyssey* III 490]. Or there are the few lines about Teuthras in *Iliad* VI:

> Then Diomedes killed Axylos, the son of Teuthras. . . . He was a
> wealthy man and friendly, for his house was beside the road and he
> gave hospitality to all men. [*Iliad* VI 12–15.]

Odysseus, of course, is quite frank about his desire to receive guest-gifts:

> 'Lord Alcinous, if you suggested that I should stay here for a full
> year and guaranteed me a safe journey home and gave me splendid
> gifts, then I should be delighted; it would be much better for me

to go home with my pockets full, for then the inhabitants of Ithaca would respect me more and I should be more popular.' [*Odyssey* XI 355–61.]

But his son Telemachus soon learns. At the start of his travels he is clearly inexperienced and nervous but at the Spartan court only a few days later, when Menelaus offers him three horses and a chariot, he tactfully declines – Ithaca is too rugged and mountainous for horses – and asks for something he can take with him more easily. Menelaus is amused by his answer and offers him instead a magnificent gold and silver bowl which he had been given by the King of Sidon. The fact that it came from so important a source added, of course, to its value as a gift. Another example of a gift with a pedigree is the boar's tusk helmet which Odysseus wore on the night attack in *Iliad* X.

Autolycus had once stolen it from Amyntor, the son of Ormenus from Eleon . . . and gave it to Amphidamas of Cythera; he gave it to Molon as a guest-gift, and Molon gave it to his son Meriones. [*Iliad* X 266–70.]

Class solidarity among the aristocrats

Kinship and guest-friendship help to bind together members of the aristocratic class and to counteract the competitive pressures of the heroic world. Loyalty within the family and friendship between members of different families must have existed in all classes of society, but they only have 'political' importance among the heroes of the aristocratic class. They encourage a feeling of class solidarity among the aristocrats and make the difference between nobles and non-nobles the most important social distinction in the Homeric world. The Homeric heroes felt that they formed a social class quite separate from the others. They had their own way of life and many privileges and they were determined to preserve them.

Two incidents involving Odysseus illustrate the point. In *Iliad* II Agamemnon calls the entire army to a meeting and, to test their morale, suggests an immediate return to Greece. He is taken at his word, and the meeting breaks up in haste as the men run down to the ships with delight. Only the prompt action of Odysseus saves the situation; whenever he met one of the nobles he tried persuasion:

'It is not appropriate for you to show fear like a commoner. . . . You do not yet clearly understand Agamemnon's purpose.'

But when he met one of the common people he struck him and upbraided him:

'Sit down and don't move. Just obey your betters, you feeble coward. You're useless in war and useless in council.' [*Iliad* II 188–206.]

When the army was seated once more and silent, there was one commoner who continued to complain about Agamemnon. This was Thersites,

> the ugliest man who came to Troy. He was bandy-legged and lame in one foot, his shoulders were hunched forward and nearly met across his chest, and his head was pointed with just a few stubbly hairs on top. [*Iliad* II 216–19.]

(Physical beauty, of course, is a characteristic of heroes.) Odysseus went across to him, spoke angrily to him and beat him over the back and shoulders – a popular move, for the army laughed at Thersites and praised Odysseus. In venturing to criticise Agamemnon Thersites may be the first figure in the development of Greek democracy, but he has no supporters. As a whole the common people are quite content to leave the direction of affairs in the hands of the aristocrats.

The common people

The main characters of the *Iliad* and *Odyssey*, and indeed most of the subordinate characters, are nobles, and when we try to find out about the common people we soon discover that there is very little evidence. It is possible, however, to piece together an outline picture.

The household of a noble contained besides his own family a considerable number of people of lower rank, both free and slave. Among the former, there might have been at the top of the scale men like Patroclus or Meriones; they are treated at Troy as the social equals of the other heroes and are prominent in battle, but they have not come as independent warriors leading their own men but because they were part of the regular establishment of Achilles and Idomeneus and were expected to obey their orders. Eteonus, who received Telemachus on his arrival at Menelaus' palace in Sparta, or the young men who poured water for the ritual of hand-washing before a meal or carved the meat may have enjoyed a similar position. Still free and enjoying some respect came the court bards, men such as Phemius and Demodocus, and the heralds. There may have been other free men below them, but we hear nothing of them, and the majority of the work force, particularly among the women, were slaves.

Slaves

Slavery played a much smaller part in Homeric Greece than it did later. Most of the slaves of whom we hear were women, and the major sources of supply were warfare, piracy, and kidnapping. In her lament over the dead body of her husband Hector, Andromache states plainly that slavery was the regular fate of the women of a defeated city:

> 'You who defended the city, with its wives and children, are dead; they will soon leave here in the Greek ships, and I among them.' [*Iliad* XXIV 729–32.]

(The fate of the Trojan women and their distribution as slaves and concubines to the victorious Greeks formed the subject matter of several of the tragedies written in Athens in the fifth century.) Chryseis and Briseis, the two girls about whom Agamemnon and Achilles quarrel in *Iliad* I, both became slaves when captured in Greek raids; so did the seven women whom Agamemnon promised to Achilles in his attempt to persuade him to return to the fighting in *Iliad* IX.

Even when we hear of slaves being bought, we may guess that it was piracy which brought them on the market in the first place. Odysseus' old nurse Eurycleia was bought by his father, and we are even told the price he paid – twenty oxen – but the fact that Homer mentions her father's and grandfather's names suggests that she was originally of good birth.

We meet several other of Odysseus' slaves – the loyal herdsman Philoetius and the treacherous goatherd Melanthius, for instance – but the most detailed portrait is that of the swineherd Eumaeus. He was the son of a king and was kidnapped by Phoenician sailors when only a child and eventually, like Eurycleia, bought by Odysseus' father Laertes. Anticleia, Odysseus' mother, treated him well, bringing him up in the home with her own daughter. On the daughter's marriage he left the palace to look after Odysseus' pigs. Eumaeus complains about the state Ithaca is in now since Odysseus left for Troy – Odysseus would have given him a home, some land, and a wife; Anticleia is dead now and Penelope is too troubled since the suitors moved into Odysseus' palace to take much notice of the slaves.

> 'For slaves really enjoy a chat with the mistress, finding out what's going on and having a bit to eat and drink and something good to take home to the farm as well.' [*Odyssey* XV 376–9.]

Even so, his position does not seem too bad. He is the chief swineherd, with other men working under him, and has even amassed enough money to buy a slave of his own.

A noble household

What unites all these people, slaves and free men, is that they belong to a noble household. The institutions of class, kin, and guest-friendship divided society horizontally, separating noble from non-noble; the importance of the household is that it divides society vertically, giving every member of it a recognised and secure place in society and allowing the common people some share in the glory of the nobles. The problem which Telemachus faced was not merely a question of whether he should encourage or permit his mother's remarriage. By the way they presented their claims to Penelope's hand the suitors threatened Odysseus' household – wife, property, slaves, and position of pre-eminence in Ithaca – and it was this that Telemachus was anxious to preserve.

Eumaeus' words quoted above show how strong a slave's feeling of 'belonging' could be, but the strength of the household in providing security and recognition is even more strikingly shown by some words Achilles addresses to Odysseus when they meet in Hades. Odysseus praises Achilles as the most fortunate of men, for previously he ruled among the living and now he does so among the dead. Achilles answers:

> 'Do not talk comfortingly to me of death, Odysseus. I should rather be alive and a labourer, working for some poor man with little property, than rule over all the dead.' [*Odyssey* XI 488–91.]

To contrast with his mighty position among the dead, Achilles chooses the lowest and least regarded position in society, not that of a slave – because a slave would enjoy the security of belonging to a noble household – but that of a free man with no land of his own, forced to make his living by hiring himself out as a labourer None of the institutions we have mentioned have any room for such a man.

Workers for the community

Higher in the social scale there were other free men not attached to a household whose position was more fortunate. Some might have land of their own, others might belong to the small class of craftsmen who are described in the *Odyssey* as *demiourgoi*, 'workers for the community'. These would be men who had some specialised skill which the normal farmer or peasant did not have. The particular crafts or professions mentioned under this heading in the *Odyssey* are those of soothsayer, doctor, carpenter (or builder), bard, and herald; to these one might add that of metal-smith. In the *Iliad* the doctors who serve with the Greek force are themselves of noble birth and command a contingent of fighting men, and we have already seen that in other parts of the *Odyssey* the bard and herald are members of a noble household. These facts suggest that when Homer refers to them as independent craftsmen working for the community in general he is referring to a later development when the importance of the household had begun to decline.

Social changes: the community

The institutions of the Greek heroic age – kinship, guest-friendship, class, household – all excluded at least some members of the community. Yet we know that the heroic age did not last for ever and that a more inclusive form of social organisation, the *polis*, gradually became normal in most of the Greek world (see Chapter 6). Are there any other signs of this change in the poems to add to the phrase 'workers for the community' mentioned in the last paragraph?

One of the standard institutions of the *polis* was an assembly in which matters of general interest to the community could be considered. In the *Iliad*, the army meets in assembly on several occasions, but the mass of the soldiers express no opinion and have no influence at all on the conduct of affairs. In the *Odyssey*, however, there are two passages where the assembly seems more important. In Book II Telemachus knows that he is not powerful enough to compel the suitors to leave his house on his own and so he calls a meeting of the assembly in the hope of persuading the Ithacans to support him. In the course of the debate, though, he is forced to admit that the trouble the suitors bring is a private one and does not really affect the community as a whole. Because of this his appeal fails. [*Odyssey* II 1–259].

Despite this, the suitors are alarmed by Telemachus' journey to Pylos and Sparta and decide to lay an ambush against his life on his return voyage. He slips past them and reaches Ithaca in safety. When the suitors discover this, they hold a meeting. Antinous urges immediate action to prevent Telemachus calling an assembly:

> 'For I'm sure he will call one soon. He will stand up in the middle of the assembly and angrily explain how we plotted to murder him but failed. The people will not like this . . . and I am afraid they may injure us or drive us into exile.' [*Odyssey*, XVI 377–81.]

Antinous realised that by plotting to murder Telemachus the suitors had gone too far; they had turned what was once a private feud into a matter of general interest which affected the whole community. The ordinary people of Ithaca preferred not to get involved in the quarrels of the nobles, but this passage shows that they sometimes felt they had a right to express an opinion and to intervene.

One other passage deserves mention. In *Iliad* XVIII Hephaestus makes some new armour for Achilles, to replace that which Hector took from the body of Patroclus. The chief piece of equipment is the shield, on which Hephaestus lavishes all his skill. He inlays the bronze with gold and silver to produce various scenes – of the constellations, of peace and war, of hunting and dancing, of ploughing, reaping, and the vine-harvest. Among them is the following:

> On it he put two splendid cities. In one of them there were weddings and scenes of feasting. The brides were being led from their homes in a torchlight procession through the city, and the sound of the marriage hymn rose around them. Young men were dancing and whirling about to the music of flutes and lyres, while the women all stood in their doorways and gazed at the sight in admiration. Meanwhile the people had gathered in the town square where two men were arguing about the blood-price for a man who had been killed. One of them was publicly offering to pay it in full; the other refused to accept it at all. They were both eager for an arbitrator to settle the affair. Each had a band of supporters and the people cheered them on. Heralds were keeping the people in order. The old men were seated in the sacred circle on benches of polished stone and held in their hands heralds' staffs. The two men came quickly up to them and each presented his case in turn. [*Iliad* XVIII 490–506.]

The kind of quarrel pictured here would once have led to a blood feud between the two families and to a situation in which the murderer could only save his life by going into exile – this, according to his story to Athena, is how Odysseus was forced to leave Crete (see beginning of this chapter). Now, when the murderer and the other man, presumably a member of the murdered man's family, disagree, there is a regular procedure sanctified by the community for settling their difference. The elders have special seats reserved for them in an area which is considered sacred, and despite all the confusion and shouting there are heralds to bring a touch of formality to the proceedings. Both in the law-suit and in the picture of the wedding we may feel that the community has come into its own and the heroic age is over.

4

Homer and the Gods

In the previous chapter we saw that there was a good deal of evidence about the heroes and the aristocratic classes, very little about those lower in the social scale. We find a similar situation when we start to consider the gods. Most of the evidence in the *Iliad* and *Odyssey* concerns the major, 'Olympian', gods and their relations with the heroes.

The Olympians

This is not really surprising when we realise that Homer thinks of these gods as a kind of super-aristocracy, standing above the heroes in much the same way as the heroes stand above the common people. He sees them as 'anthropomorphic' (Greek *anthropos* = man, *morphe* = shape); they have the physical appearance of humans and also possess human emotions, but differ from them in being vastly more powerful. They are worshipped not because they represent any higher form of morality or can inspire men to better lives but simply for that power. In just the same way the commoners did not expect their social superiors to be better men than they were themselves but they continued to look up to them and respect them because they possessed far greater power and it could be dangerous not to acknowledge this openly. Sarpedon well understood this parallel between the world of gods and that of men when he pointed out to Glaucus that the Lycians honoured them 'like gods'.

At the same time there are close links between the human and divine aristocracies – most obviously, those of family relationship. Many of the heroic families traced their ancestry back to a divine origin. Achilles is the son of the mortal Peleus and the sea-goddess Thetis, whom Zeus himself once thought of marrying; Helen is the daughter of Zeus and the mortal Leda; the Trojan leader Aeneas is the son of Anchises and the goddess Aphrodite, who intervenes in the fighting to save her son from death at the hands of Diomedes; in the dual between Sarpedon and Tlepolemus Zeus is involved on both sides, for the former is his son and the latter his grandson.

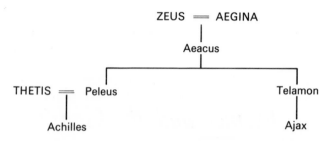

The families of Achilles and Ajax, showing how gods (in capital letters) and mortals were interrelated.

But though the gods are linked to the world of men in this way, there are certain respects in which they differ from mere mortals. In their veins flows not blood but *ichor*, their food is *ambrosia* and their drink *nectar*. At times they even seem to speak another language, as for example when Hermes gives Odysseus the magic root which will protect him from Circe's wiles: 'the gods call it *moly*' [*Odyssey* x 305]. They live a life of serene splendour on Mount Olympus,

> where men say the home of the gods is fixed, secure for ever; it is not buffeted by winds nor drenched by rain or snow, but around it spreads a clear, cloudless sky which gleams with a bright light. [*Odyssey* VI 42–5.]

In their human shape the gods are normally visible to men but they can if they wish cloak themselves, or their favourites, in a kind of mist and so become invisible. Normally too they are described, when they intervene in the action of the poems, in purely human terms but on certain occasions Homer goes beyond this to reveal their divine power and strength. Ares' battle-cry is as loud as ten thousand men, and when he falls to the ground, wounded by Athena, his body stretches over two hundred yards.

But for all their power the gods are not all-powerful. To begin with, the very fact that Homer sees them in anthropomorphic terms imposes certain restrictions. Glaucus may say in prayer to Apollo

> 'Listen to me, lord, whether you are in the rich land of Lycia or in Troy; for you can hear a man in trouble wherever you are.' [*Iliad* XVI 513–15.]

But elsewhere in the poems Homer speaks as though the gods are limited by considerations of time and space in just the same way as mortals. An example of this occurs in *Iliad* I. Achilles urges Thetis to tell Zeus how he has been treated by Agamemnon but she explains that she will not be able to do this for twelve days as Zeus and the other gods have gone to a banquet in the land of the Ethiopians and will not be back till then. In the story of the love of Ares and Aphrodite which Demodocus sings at the

Phaeacian court (*Odyssey* VIII) Hephaestus pretends to be going on a journey to Lemnos because he knows that Ares will seize this opportunity to go to bed with Aphrodite and that he will thus be able to catch them in the net which he has so cunningly made. A final illustration of the point may be taken from a critical moment in the *Iliad* (Book XIV). When the tide of battle turns against the Greeks Poseidon intervenes to help them, but it looks for a moment as if Zeus may order him to leave the battlefield. Hera sets out to seduce Zeus so that when they have made love he will fall asleep and Poseidon will thus be left free to continue his assistance to the Greeks.

Secondly, the other gods are limited by the superior power of Zeus. Here again we can see the parallel with the human situation; the Greek heroes all have wills and intentions of their own but they accept, if sometimes reluctantly, the superior position of Agamemnon. Similarly, the other gods may go against Zeus' wishes, particularly when they think they can do so safely, but when they receive a direct order they obey. In *Iliad* VIII, Hera and Athena set off to help the Greeks in battle; a message from Zeus makes them change their mind. Hera herself, the most bitter in her attitude to·Zeus, admits that his power is supreme among the gods [*Iliad* XV 107–8] and Zeus' own brother, Poseidon, says plainly that he would not be prepared to join the other gods in opposing him, 'for he is much stronger'. [*Iliad* VIII 211.]

Zeus

This makes it appropriate to start with Zeus when we turn to consider some of the individual Olympians in more detail. His position of pre-eminence may also account for the fact that he does not intervene in the events of the human world in the same way as other gods. When Apollo's priest, Chryses, is insulted by Agamemnon in *Iliad* I, Apollo punishes the Greek army by sending a plague and later he fights himself on the Trojan side and is responsible for Patroclus' death, but Zeus uses much less direct methods. He may send a dream, as he does to Agamemnon in *Iliad* II, or allow his will to be known from omens:

> Zeus had pity for Agamemnon's tears and gave a nod to show that his army would not be destroyed. He sent the most reliable bird of prophecy, an eagle, holding in its claws a fawn. The eagle dropped the fawn beside the splendid altar where the Greeks used to sacrifice to Zeus the Giver of Oracles. When the Greeks saw that the bird came from Zeus, they rushed at the Trojans with greater enthusiasm. [*Iliad* VIII 245–52.]

Frequently he intervenes by sending one of his divine messengers; in

Iliad VIII it is Iris who carries the message telling Hera and Athena not to join in the fighting, and in *Odyssey* V Zeus sends Hermes to order Calypso to allow Odysseus to leave her island.

Nevertheless, it is Zeus who controls the course of events in both poems. At the council of gods in *Odyssey* I and V he gives Athena permission to bring about Odysseus' return to Ithaca. In the *Iliad* his hand is even more evident, for the whole plot of the poem is the working out of Zeus' plan for making the Greeks restore to Achilles the honour he has lost as a result of Agamemnon's behaviour in *Iliad* I. In *Iliad* IV Zeus indirectly encourages the Trojans to break the truce which might have brought the war to an end; in *Iliad* VIII he orders the gods not to take part in the fighting so that the Trojan success will continue unimpeded; in *Iliad* XV he outlines his plan for Patroclus' entry into the battle, his death, Achilles' return to the fighting, and the death of Hector; and in *Iliad* XXIV he explains that Thetis must persuade Achilles to give back the body of Hector to Priam.

But not even Zeus is all-powerful. Beside him there is the power of Fate, or Destiny. At times Homer seems to speak as though Zeus and Fate are one and the same or even that Zeus controls or carries out the decrees of Fate. In the scene of the duel between Achilles and Hector in *Iliad* XXII Zeus is described as weighing in his golden scales the fates of the two heroes; Hector's was the heavier, and his doom was sealed. However, other incidents reveal a more fatalistic attitude which believed that the day of a man's death was fixed independently of Zeus and that he was expected not to try to alter it. In *Iliad* XVI, for example, Zeus would like to save his son Sarpedon from death at Patroclus' hands, but on Hera's advice he refrains from interfering.

Athena

Athena plays a prominent part in both poems. She prevents Achilles drawing his sword on Agamemnon in *Iliad* I, she encourages Diomedes in the first day's fighting, and she is constant in her support of the Greek cause. One incident in which she is involved is worth describing in greater detail. In *Iliad* XXII, when Achilles and Hector finally meet, Achilles chases Hector round the walls of Troy. Athena takes on the appearance of Hector's brother Deiphobus and encourages him to stand and face Achilles. When Achilles throws his spear Hector ducks and it passes harmlessly over him, but Athena picks it up and returns it to Achilles. Then Hector hurls his spear; it strikes full in the middle of Achilles' shield but cannot pierce it. He turns to Deiphobus for another spear.

But he was nowhere there. Hector realised what had happened and said 'It is true then, the gods called me to my death. I thought Deiphobus was at my side but he is in Troy; Athena deceived me. My death is now at hand.' [*Iliad* XXII 295–300.]

It is in the *Odyssey*, though, that Athena really comes into her own. If Odysseus is the hero, she is almost the heroine of the poem. Throughout it she acts as patron to Odysseus and his family, protecting them and aiding them in every way. It is she who brings up the question of Odysseus' return before the council of the gods and reminds Zeus of his promises when he seems to have forgotten them. She brings Odysseus to Scheria and persuades the Phaeacians to help him. Once in Ithaca she joins Odysseus and reveals herself to him. Together they plot vengeance on the suitors. She makes Penelope suggest the trial of strength by the bow and she stands by Odysseus during the battle with the suitors, turning their javelins from her favourite. Similarly with Telemachus. She tells him how to address the assembly in Ithaca and reminds him that he has reached years of discretion. She sends him to Pylos and Sparta and she brings him home again. She screws up his courage by exposing him to the taunts of the suitors and encourages him just before the fight in the palace.

But these are major incidents. It is astonishing in what detail Athena helps this family; nothing is too insignificant for her. She suddenly appears among the Phaeacians to mark the spot where Odysseus' discus has fallen; she acts as guide to Odysseus and Telemachus; she thinks of Penelope's grief at Telemachus' absence; she even plays the housemaid and carries a light for Odysseus and Eurycleia. She looks after Odysseus' disguises and so frequently brings sleep to the eyes of her favourites that we are not surprised when we reach *Odyssey* XXIII to find that they cannot even wake unaided.

Aphrodite

Aphrodite sometimes seems a rather feeble figure. In *Iliad* V Athena warns Diomedes not to attack any of the gods – except Aphrodite. When she does enter the fighting to protect her son Aeneas, Diomedes leaps into the attack and wounds her on the wrist. Aphrodite screams in terror and rapidly leaves the battlefield for Olympus. There she protests about Diomedes' assault on a god, but her complaints receive little sympathy. Hera and Athena openly mock her, and even Zeus does not take the matter very seriously.

> The father of gods and men smiled and called to Aphrodite, saying 'Warfare is not for you, my child – Ares and Athena will look after that; your task is with matters of desire and marriage.' [*Iliad* V 426–30.]

And in fact when we see Aphrodite in her role as goddess of love and desire, there is no doubting her divine power. In *Iliad* III a duel is arranged between Menelaus and Paris. At first Paris shrinks back in fear and Hector rebukes him for his effeminacy and cowardice, referring sarcastically to his long hair and lyre and to the 'gifts of Aphrodite'. Paris accepts the justice of the rebuke but adds

> 'Do not reproach me for the lovely gifts of golden Aphrodite. The gifts of the gods are not to be despised'. [*Iliad* III, 64–5.]

Later, when the duel begins, Menelaus rapidly gains the upper hand. Even though his sword breaks, he hurls himself at Paris, grabs hold of him by the crest of his helmet, and starts to drag him back to the Greek ships.

> And he would have succeeded and won great glory if Aphrodite had not quickly noticed it. She broke the leather strap of the helmet and it came away in Menelaus' hand. He threw it to the Greeks . . . and leapt after Paris, longing to kill him with his spear. But Aphrodite snatched him away with great ease, as a god can, and hid him in a thick mist. (*Iliad* III 373–81.]

Aphrodite takes Paris back to his own bedroom and, disguised as an old woman, goes to recall Helen from the Trojan walls where she has been watching the fight.

> 'Paris summons you to return home. He is in his room on his bed, radiant with beauty and dressed in his finest clothes. You would never imagine he had just returned from battle but would think he was just going to a dance or was resting after one.' [*Iliad* III 390–4.]

Helen sees through the disguise and recognises the goddess. She refuses to return, protesting angrily:

> 'You go and sit with Paris; give up the life of a goddess, stay away from Olympus, but worry yourself about him all the time, look after him, until he makes you his wife – or his slave. I'll never go back and share his bed, it would be disgraceful.' [*Iliad* III 406–10.]

Aphrodite replies angrily:

> 'Don't provoke me, you impudent woman, or I may lose my temper and abandon you, and hate you as much as I have loved you so far.' [*Iliad* III 414–15.]

Helen is cowed into submission and follows the goddess to Paris' bedroom. Sitting opposite him on a chair placed for her by Aphrodite, she attacks Paris:

> 'You are back from battle. I wish you had died there at the hands of my former husband. There was a time once when you used to claim

you were a better warrior than Menelaus. Well, go and challenge him to another duel. No, I advise you not to . . . he may kill you.' [*Iliad* III 428–36.]

Paris replies:

'Do not reproach me. Menelaus, with Athena's help, has defeated me now; another time I shall defeat him – there are gods on my side too. But come, let us go to bed and enjoy our love. Never yet have I felt such desire and longing for you . . . as I do now.' He led the way towards the bed, and his wife followed him.

So they lay down upon the bed, and meanwhile Menelaus was prowling through the army like a wild beast, trying to catch sight of Paris. [*Iliad* III 438–50.]

The entire scene is a masterpiece of psychological insight, showing Homer's deep understanding of human nature. Both Paris and Helen are blessed – or cursed – with the 'gifts of Aphrodite', the power to arouse sexual desire. Paris knows that he is no warrior, and so accepts the justice of Hector's rebuke, but he also knows that he has other qualities which are no less god-given and when Hector criticises these, he defends himself, for he realises that he must be true to his own character. He feels no shame at the manner of his rescue from Menelaus, but dismissing the whole incident from his mind with the trite and obviously false remark that he will beat him next time he returns with relief to his own world – 'never yet have I felt such desire and longing for you . . .'. If Paris' acceptance of Aphrodite's gifts is straightforward and uncomplicated, Helen is in a more difficult position. She is torn between revulsion from Paris, especially now he has proved inferior to her former husband on the field of battle, and desire for him. She tries to fight against her desire but finds it too strong for her. Homer's belief in anthropomorphic gods makes it possible for him to present these emotions externally, through the power and personality of the goddess Aphrodite, and to do so in a particularly vivid and dramatic manner.

Aphrodite's function is to be the goddess of love and desire. Similarly, Ares is the god of war and Apollo, among other things, the god of prophecy, while it has been suggested that one aspect of Athena's role in the poems is as the goddess of success. This suggestion would explain why she is with Achilles when he kills Hector. To us the contest seems unfair, two against one, but Athena is not there because Achilles needs her aid but simply as an indication that he is bound to win. It is a way of making us see the inevitability of his success. The suggestion would also explain her support for Diomedes in the scenes of his battle success in *Iliad* V and VI and her unflagging concern for that born winner Odysseus.

10. *Hephaestus, the blacksmith of the gods. Thetis asks Hephaestus to make new armour for Achilles.* [*Iliad* XVIII]

Homer's attitude to the gods

The modern reader is often surprised to discover that Homer's attitude to the gods seems remarkably lacking in reverence. He admits their super-human power, but otherwise describes them in very similar terms to those he uses for his mortal characters. At times indeed he comes close to ridiculing them, though this is almost always confined to scenes where we see the gods alone. One example of this is Hera's seduction of Zeus in *Iliad* XIV; another, perhaps even more striking, is the brilliant story of the love of Ares and Aphrodite which Demodocus tells in *Odyssey* VIII. In this and also on two occasions in the *Iliad*, when he attempts to reconcile the quarrelling gods in Book I and when Thetis calls on him to order new armour for Achilles in Book XVIII, the hobbling figure of Hephaestus is treated with little respect – mere snobbery perhaps, for he was only a blacksmith. Particularly in the scenes where Aphrodite and Ares retreat from Diomedes there is a lack of dignity in the behaviour of the gods which we never find among the humans.

By keeping his narrative on a human scale Homer makes it easier for his audience to enter the world of the heroes and share their experiences. We should find it more difficult to do this if he used magic and the supernatural too frequently or too obviously. It is because Homer only rarely departs from the natural course of events that passages like the one at the end of *Iliad* XIX seem so impressive. Achilles has reproved his horses for being too slow to bring Patroclus back safely from the battle. One of the horses, Xanthus, is given the power of speech.

> He lowered his head to the ground and his mane came tumbling forward from the yoke. He spoke to Achilles: 'Certainly we shall save you this time, mighty Achilles, but the day of your death is near at hand.' [*Iliad* XIX 405–9.]

Minor divinities

In the *Odyssey* the number of minor divinities is greater. They range from the beautiful goddesses Circe and Calypso, through the monstrous Laestrygonians, to such mythical creatures as Scylla and Charybdis, and the magical element obviously plays a greater part than in the *Iliad*. Even in the *Odyssey*, though, Homer is careful not to overdo it. We can accept a degree of the supernatural in Odysseus' story of his wanderings which we should consider out of place in Ithaca. Even the one-eyed monster Polyphemus is really quite human – thoroughly uncivilised, of course, but basically not very different from the rest of us. He looks after his flocks with care, even perhaps with pride, and however much we wish to see him outwitted and rejoice at Odysseus' escape we can appreciate his feelings as he speaks to his prize ram when it leaves the cave carrying Odysseus.

> 'Dear ram, why are you the last of the flock to leave the cave? You have never been last before. You always used to step out at the head of the flock – first to crop the sweet grass, first to reach the flowing streams, and first in your eagerness to return to the pen in the evening. But now you are last of all. Are you grieving because your master is now blind? It was that wicked Noman with his cursed companions who did it – he made me drunk and then put out my eye. But he hasn't escaped death yet. If only you could feel as I do and could speak and tell me where he's hiding from my

11. *Odysseus and Polyphemus's ram: 'Last of the flock to go up to the door was the ram, burdened by the weight of his fleece and me.'* [*Odyssey* IX 444–45]

anger! Then I'd bash his brains out on the ground, spattering them all over the cave. That way I should feel some relief from the pain which that good-for-nothing Noman has caused me.' [*Odyssey* IX 447–60.]

Changes in religious attitudes

In the previous chapter we noticed signs that the aristocratic world of the heroes was giving way to a society in which the community as a whole had some rights and an established way of expressing them. We began this chapter by drawing a parallel between those heroes and the Olympian gods, who were worshipped not for their moral qualities but for their power. Is there any evidence that religious attitudes were changing in a similar way?

Zeus is sometimes described in the poems as 'god of strangers' and 'god of suppliants'. It must have been obvious that these two classes of people needed protection. What is significant is that men then began to expect the gods to act as moral policemen, enforcing human rules of conduct. Of all the quarrelsome Olympians only Zeus, the most powerful, could be sufficiently impartial to administer these rules fairly, and so it was to him that such functions were assigned. The idea that the gods are interested in problems of right and wrong and do not intervene except when their descendants or favourites are involved, is more evident in the *Odyssey* than the *Iliad*, but a similar, comparatively advanced, view of the gods can be seen in the following lines from *Iliad* XVI:

Just as when the rain beats down heavily upon the earth in autumn, when Zeus is angry with men who deliver crooked judgements in the town square, overturning justice and ignoring the vengeance of the gods. . . . [*Iliad* XVI 384–8.]

We can now see beyond the law-suit pictured on the shield of Achilles (Chapter 3 above). One reason why the two men quarrelling over the blood-price were prepared to bring their case to arbitration was that they and the old men seated in their sacred circle in the town square had come to believe that Zeus was watching such scenes and would be angry if justice were not done.

5

Homer and the Poems

Characterisation

A MODERN novelist may make use of various methods to portray character. He can, for example, describe a man's external appearance – his height, the way he walks, the clothes he wears; he can penetrate inside the character's mind, revealing to the reader his feelings, ambitions of which the other characters in the book may know nothing, even his unconscious fears and desires; and he can indicate by the way he does this his attitude to the character, showing whether he approves or disapproves of him.

None of these methods is common in Homer. There is very little direct description of individual characteristics; the comparatively detailed picture of the misshapen Thersites is almost unique, and it is a commonplace that Homer nowhere describes Helen's beauty but merely allows us to over-hear the comments of the old men of Troy (*Iliad* III 154–8). He hardly ever tells us directly what a character feels, and it is only very rarely that he shows what he thinks about a character's behaviour.

His method is very different from these. He portrays the character of his heroes by presenting them to us in action, so that we see what they do and hear what they say, thus allowing us to make up our own minds about them.

Achilles

The most fully developed of the characters Homer portrays is Achilles, who despite his absence from much of the action is the central figure of the *Iliad*. The keynote of his character is established in the very first line of the poem: 'Sing, Muse, of the *anger* of Achilles . . .'.

When he calls a meeting of the Assembly to discover why Apollo has sent a plague upon the Greeks, Achilles is quick-spirited in the traditional heroic way. When Agamemnon selfishly refuses to give up the girl Chryseis without recompense, Achilles too becomes angry. Both heroes lose their tempers, but Achilles' anger is generous and public-spirited, and it is Agamemnon who is the more deeply in the wrong. He publicly insults Achilles' honour by taking Briseis from him, and when Achilles then decides to withdraw from the fighting our sympathies go with him.

During his absence from battle Achilles reflects upon the heroic moral code by which he has lived so far and in particular upon the choice of destiny which his mother Thetis has foretold for him – either a short glorious life and death at Troy or a long, inglorious life at home in Greece. Thus, by the time Agamemnon can bring himself to try to make up the quarrel by offering Achilles generous gifts and decides to send ambassadors to tell him this Achilles has come close to rejecting the heroic moral code.

Sarpedon claimed that he was prepared to risk his life in battle because of the honours the Lycians paid him, but Achilles can feel no such confidence, for, as he states in his reply to Odysseus, the first of Agamemnon's ambassadors to speak:

'The coward and the noble warrior receive equal honour. Death makes no distinction between the man with no achievements to his credit and the man with many. I have toiled hard and have always ventured my life in battle, but I have gained nothing by it.' [*Iliad* IX 319–22.]

His dissatisfaction with the heroic code makes Agamemnon's offer meaningless, and he rejects it utterly. By so doing he puts himself entirely in the wrong in the eyes of the other Greek heroes. Even Achilles' own troops, the Myrmidons, and his friend Patroclus criticise him.

When the Trojans reach the ships and the Greek plight seems desperate, Achilles himself realises that he cannot nurse his grievance for ever and when Patroclus asks to borrow his armour and lead the Myrmidons to the rescue, he agrees. When he hears that Hector has killed Patroclus, his grief is inconsolable. The lingering resentment he still feels against Agamemnon flares up again into passionate anger, directed now against Hector, an anger that can be quenched only by Hector's death. Yet for all his black determination to kill Hector, Achilles is now aware of his own character in a way that was not true before; he says to his mother Thetis:

'How I wish that quarrelling and anger might vanish from the world of gods and men. It makes even a sensible man violent, it rises in a man's heart like smoke and its taste is sweeter than honey.' [*Iliad* XVIII 107–10.]

This self-consciousness separates Achilles from the other heroes and will continue to do so throughout the poem.

When he enters the battle again, Achilles is utterly ruthless, rejecting appeals for mercy that, as he admits himself, he would have accepted previously. Yet he does not take the sort of pleasure in his success that

12. *Achilles and Hector: the duel from* Iliad XXII *as seen by a vase painter of about* 500 B.C.

Diomedes does in Books v and vi, but regards it merely as a duty he owes the ghost of Patroclus. His anger is still full as he kills Hector – he wishes he could bring himself to cut him up and eat him – and goes on to drag the corpse round the walls of Troy behind his chariot. This action calls from Homer one of his rare personal comments on the behaviour of his characters; it is 'disgraceful'. Another comes shortly after, as Achilles conducts the funeral of Patroclus and sacrifices twelve Trojan captives at his pyre – 'an evil deed'.

Nevertheless, once the funeral is complete, we see Achilles beginning to take part once more in the social activities of the Greeks. He presides over the funeral games courteously and with authority. But he has not yet given up his anger, for he continues to drag Hector daily round the walls of Troy. On the twelfth day King Priam resolves to venture into the Greek camp by night and to ransom back the body of Hector for burial. He enters Achilles' tent, and going up to him kisses the hands that have killed his son and appeals to him in the name of his father Peleus. Moved by the sight of the old man and by the mention of his own father – for he knows that he is fated now to die at Troy and never see him again – Achilles

> gently pushed the old man from him with his hand. Priam lay crouching at Achilles' feet and wept as he remembered Hector, while Achilles wept now for his father, now for Patroclus. [*Iliad* XXIV 508–11.]

These tears and his sympathy for the plight of Priam bring Achilles' anger to its end. The plot of the *Iliad* is now over. Achilles' character has not changed – a moment later he breaks out furiously against Priam – but it has developed and, above all, he has grown in self-knowledge. It is his tragedy that this could only be acquired by the intense suffering he experiences in the poem.

Techniques of story-telling

The most basic skill a bard needed was the ability to tell a story in a way which kept the interest of his audience. Without this, other virtues such as skill in characterisation would count for little. The importance of this skill becomes even greater when we consider the enormous length of the *Iliad* and *Odyssey* and the fact that they are not just straightforward stories of heroic action of the type with which the bards were most familiar: for the *Iliad* sets a story of individual tragedy against a background of heroic society, while the *Odyssey* not only consists of two strands – the stories of Odysseus and Telemachus – which are first kept separate and then combined but also involves a lengthy 'flashback' in Odysseus' narrative to the Phaeacians.

(a) Variety

One of the techniques a bard can use to sustain interest in his story is variety. In the *Odyssey* this is of many kinds. Homer tells much of the poem in his own person but he also employs a number of other narrators. Apart from Odysseus himself, both in his account of his wanderings and in his various lying stories, Nestor talks about the war at Troy and his return to Greece, Menelaus tells the story of his adventures in Egypt on the way home from Troy, Eumaeus describes how he became a slave, and Demodocus recounts the story of Ares and Aphrodite.

The types of incident in the poem also vary. Odysseus' lying stories are simple and almost historical in feeling, while the slaughter of the suitors shows a typically heroic delight in battle and bloodshed. Quite different is the feeling of magic and fantasy that surrounds some of Odysseus' adventures at sea. Different again are the sophistication of Demodocus' poem or the scene in Book IV where Helen and Menelaus – like any other happily married couple – vie with each other in dragging up the past, and the sensitivity and humour with which Homer handles the relations between Odysseus and Nausicaa. It is easy to understand why the *Odyssey* is sometimes described as the earliest novel in European literature.

At first sight the success of the *Iliad* seems to owe less to variety than does that of the *Odyssey*, yet the very fact that so much of the poem is taken up with scenes of battle makes what variety there is all the more important.

The scenes on Olympus may sometimes provide a variety welcome for its own sake – as the wounding of Aphrodite and its consequences (*Iliad* v) occurs in the middle of Diomedes' exploits or Hera's seduction of Zeus (*Iliad* XIV) interrupts the Trojan attack on the Greek ships – but some of the scenes in Troy, particularly those involving Hector and Andromache, have the more serious purpose of allowing us to see the effect the war has on the people of Troy.

Homer introduces many short, sharply detailed pictures of ordinary life into his narrative, and these have a similar effect. Sometimes he singles out one from among a list of the victims of some great hero and gives just enough extra information for us to see him as a person – Axylus, for example, who was killed by Diomedes and whose father 'lived beside the road and gave hospitality to all men', or Hippothous, who perished in the battle over the body of Patroclus 'far from fertile Larissa and could not repay his parents for the way they looked after him when he was a child'.

Many others occur in the similes which are such an obvious feature of the poems. The great warrior Ajax, slowly and stubbornly retreating before the Trojans, is compared first to a lion and then to a donkey which leaves the path to go into a field and stays there munching the crops and ignoring all the efforts of the boys to drive it out until it has eaten enough (*Iliad* XI, 556–61). When Menelaus is wounded, the sight of the blood gives rise to the picture of a woman staining ivory with purple to make the cheek-piece for a horse (*Iliad* IV 141–5).

Or there is the magnificent simile which Homer uses at the end of Book VIII to illustrate the appearance of the Trojan camp fires dotted over the plain by night.

> It was like a night when the air is calm and still and the stars shine brightly in the sky about the clear moon. You can make out all the peaks and the ridges jutting out from the mountains and the valleys between them and can see right up through the sky to heaven above and all the stars. The shepherd rejoices to see it. [*Iliad* VIII 555–9.]

Many of the details in these pictures are probably traditional, but it is Homer who has chosen them and fitted them so skilfully into his story. They remind the audience that there are areas of human life with which the main narrative of the *Iliad* does not deal and so put the battle scenes into perspective.

(b) Suspense

A second weapon the bard can use is suspense. Many modern books or films are exciting because we want to find out what happens next. Since Homer's audience probably knew the outline of the stories of the *Iliad* and *Odyssey*, this type of suspense is not so important in them. Instead, Homer could arouse his audience's excitement by making them wonder just *how* an episode would end – how, for example, Odysseus would escape from yet another seemingly impossible situation.

We can see how Homer uses this technique at several stages in the story of Odysseus' encounter with the Cyclops in *Odyssey* IX.

Odysseus has twelve of his men with him when they enter the Cyclops' cave. They would like to make off quickly with some of the sheep and any of the food they can easily carry, but Odysseus insists on waiting to see the owner of the cave. When the Cyclops arrives they are terrified, and we begin to wonder just how he will treat them. But Homer does not tell us immediately. He makes us wait, sharing the Greeks' fright as they cower in a corner of the cave, while he describes the Cyclops' methodical milking of the sheep and goats and how he curdled half of the milk for cheese and left half standing in the pails. Only after all this does the Cyclops notice Odysseus and his men.

The Cyclops eats two of Odysseus' men for supper and two more for breakfast the next morning. Eight remain. During the day, while the Cyclops is out with his flocks, Odysseus works out his plan for making the Cyclops drunk and blinding him while he sleeps. For the scheme to work Odysseus needs the help of four of his men. When the Cyclops comes home that evening he eats two more of Odysseus' men. Only six now remain – and if Odysseus does not succeed that night he is doomed, for in twenty-four hours he will have only two companions and will be unable to carry out the scheme.

All goes well, however. The Cyclops falls into a drunken sleep, vomiting out some of the wine and half-digested morsels of the flesh of Odysseus' unlucky companions. Odysseus heats the great pole in the ashes of the fire and then his men

> 'drove it right into the middle of the Cyclops' eye. I pressed down on it from above and twisted it, like a ships' carpenter boring a hole in a plank of wood with a drill, while below him on each side his mates pull at thongs of leather to keep it turning, and the drill runs smoothly in the hole. That was just the way we worked as we twisted the stake in his eye. The point of the stake was red-hot and the blood ran out all round it. His eyebrows and eyelids were all burnt, the eyeball caught fire, and the roots of the eye hissed in the heat. It was the sort of sharp hiss you hear when a blacksmith dips an axe in cold water to temper it – that's how he makes the iron strong. This was the sound that came from his eye as it sizzled around the stake. He shrieked aloud. . . .' [*Odyssey* IX 382–95.]

In fact, of course, the Cyclops shrieked as soon as he felt the hot stake in his eye, but Homer slows down the narrative – it is like a film going into

13. *The blinding of Polyphemus by Odysseus and his men.*

slow motion – and makes us linger over this moment of triumph. The audience is already excited by the story. The two similes prolong that excitement, as the audience recognises the familiar pictures of a ships' carpenter and a blacksmith at work. The blinding of a one-eyed monster, which could so easily seem strange and unnatural, suddenly becomes something which every member of the audience can understand and appreciate from his own experience.

Next morning the Cyclops moves away the great stone from the door of the cave and Odysseus and his surviving companions escape with the flocks and make their way back to their ship. They cast off and start rowing. But Odysseus cannot resist the opportunity of taunting the

Cyclops. Guided by the sound of his voice, the Cyclops breaks off the peak of a mountain and hurls it at Odysseus and his men. It falls just in front of the ship, and the wave it causes drives the ship back to land. Odysseus' refusal to keep his mouth shut has brought them straight back into danger. Odysseus pushes the boat off again and the crew row hard. When they have gone about twice as far from the land as they had before, Odysseus proposes to yell at the Cyclops again. His men try to restrain him, but in vain.

> 'Cyclops, if anyone asks you how you lost the sight of your eye, tell them it was Odysseus who did it – Odysseus the sacker of cities, the son of Laertes, who lives in Ithaca.' [*Odyssey* IX 502–5.]

Again Homer makes us wonder how things will turn out. Where will this new folly land Odysseus and his men? We wait, as the Cyclops curses Odysseus and then hurls another rock at his ship. It lands just behind the ship, and the wave it causes drives the ship out to sea. Odysseus has escaped again.

(c) Structure

But however much variety or suspense a bard may put into his poem, it will not be a real success unless its structure is right. The audience may enjoy each of the individual scenes but still not feel that they add up. The order in which incidents occur, the amount of attention the poet gives them, the pace he chooses for telling them – these make up the structure of the poem. For the structure to be a success, the audience must feel as it listens to the poem that the separate parts all contribute to a total effect.

On a small scale it is not difficult to appreciate Homer's skill at arranging incidents. In the *Odyssey*, the story of the Cyclops is told at some length and with a good deal of vivid detail. It is followed by two much shorter episodes – Odysseus' visit to Aeolus, king of the winds, and the destruction of all the ships in the fleet except his own by the Laestrygonians – before Homer moves on to another major one, the story of Odysseus and Circe.

As another illustration of this point we may take the last scene of the *Iliad*, when Priam returns from Achilles' tent with the body of Hector. The Trojans mourn his death, and the three women most affected – his wife Andromache, his mother Hecuba, and Helen – each sing a lament over him. At the end of Andromache's come the lines:

> This is what she said in her grief and the women mourned with her. Then Hecuba began her shrill lament.

When Hecuba ends, the lines are:

> This is what she said in her grief and she roused the people to unceasing lamentation. Helen was the third who began a lament.

And after Helen:

> This is what she said in her grief, and the people mourned with her. [*Iliad* XXIV 746–7, 760–1, 776].

By this repetition Homer creates a formal pattern for the laments which makes the grief seem more intense and also slows down the pace of the poem so that it comes naturally to its end.

The same care for structure can also be seen on a larger scale.

Iliad

The theme of the *Iliad* is set out in the opening lines of the poem: the anger of Achilles led to the death of many Greek heroes, and this was what Zeus intended should happen. When Achilles withdrew from the fighting he asked his mother Thetis to persuade Zeus to help him recover the honour that he had lost as a result of Agamemnon's insults. Zeus' plan was that the Greeks should be so hard pressed by the Trojans that they would be prepared to humble themselves to Achilles and beg him to re-enter the battle.

Yet the scenes of battle open with a resounding Greek success as Diomedes drives the Trojans back towards their city (Books V and VI). Why is this? Homer wants to make his audience realise how much difference the absence of Achilles made to the Greek force. If he plunged straight into a scene of Greek defeat, he would leave the audience without any standard of comparison and they would not be able to appreciate this for themselves.

On the other hand, he cannot easily include in the poem scenes of Achilles' success in battle which occurred before the action of the poem started. To overcome this difficulty Homer uses the figure of Diomedes as a substitute for Achilles. Both Achilles and Diomedes are young and brilliant warriors of a bold and daring spirit. By describing Diomedes' success and making the first day's fighting go in favour of the Greeks, Homer provides the audience with a standard of comparison against which they can measure the scenes of Greek disaster in Books VIII and XII –XV. They can now appreciate from personal experience just how utterly the Greeks collapsed when the plan of Zeus started to take effect. Without these scenes that would not have been possible.

Odyssey

We have already mentioned the two chief features of the structure of the *Odyssey* – the fact that it combines two strands, the stories of Odysseus and Telemachus, and contains a lengthy 'flashback' section. We will now look at these in more detail.

After the council of the gods at the beginning of Book I Homer concentrates on Telemachus for the first four books, but he does not allow us to forget about Odysseus. The problems which the young Telemachus faces in Ithaca are caused by Odysseus' absence; Athena, disguised as Mentor, prompts him to travel to Pylos and Sparta for news of Odysseus; and both Nestor and Menelaus speak of Odysseus' courage and resourcefulness.

At the start of Book V Homer returns to the council of the gods and then switches to the story of Odysseus. His adventures at sea are so colourful and vivid that it is perhaps rather difficult to keep Telemachus in mind all the time. Nevertheless Homer tries to stop us forgetting about him entirely by making us anxious for him; he ends Book IV with the report of the suitors' plan to ambush Telemachus on his return to Ithaca.

The events about which Odysseus tells the Phaeacians in Books IX–XII had all occurred before the action of the *Odyssey* started. They are good stories, of course, but that is not the only reason Homer includes them in the poem. Ten years had passed since the end of the Trojan War and Odysseus had still not returned to Ithaca. By making Odysseus recount the story of his adventures during that period Homer allows the audience to live through those ten years and feel the passage of time and so helps them to appreciate the troubles his long absence from Ithaca has brought to Penelope and Telemachus. The choice of a 'flashback' thus contributes directly to the total effect of the poem.

6

Homer and History

History

MOST Greeks considered that the *Iliad* and *Odyssey* were historically true and gave an accurate picture of life around the time of the Trojan War (about 1200 BC). How far would modern scholars agree with them?

Mycenaean Greece

Around 1200 Greece was divided into a number of small independent states. They were centred on strongly-built citadels, where the king had his palace and where the local population could take refuge if there was a raid or an invasion. The most famous of these is Mycenae, the citadel of Agamemnon, and for this reason this period of Greek history is generally called Mycenaean.

Mycenae
The citadel of Mycenae is situated on a spur jutting from between two mountains and dominates the plain over which it ruled. On almost every side the ground drops away sharply, but except at the steepest point the citadel is further protected by massive walls. Inside it is roughly terraced,

Line (1) ti-ri-po-de ai-ke-u ke-re-si-jo we-ke TRIPOD 2 ti-ri-po e-me po-de o-wo-we TRIP•
ke-re-a₂ no-[pe-re ? TRIPOD 1]

(2) qe-to WINE-JAR ? 3 di-pa me-zo-e qe-to-ro-we POT 1 di-pa-e me-zo-e ti-ri-o-w

(3) di-pa me-wi-jo ti-ri-jo-we POT 1 di-pa me-wi-jo a-no-we POT 1

with the palace on the summit and a small number of houses for court officials below it. Outside the citadel are traces of other houses and the road system, while both inside and outside tombs have been found. When he excavated some of these in 1876 the German archaeologist Schliemann discovered a mass of valuable and luxurious objects – gold ornaments for the dead man's clothes, jewellery of many kinds, and bronze weapons, including daggers with blades elaborately inlaid in gold and silver.

Linear B

Most of what we know about this civilisation comes from the work of archaeologists. Probably the most important of their discoveries for our knowledge of the period are the Linear B tablets. These are clay tablets found both in Crete and at several sites on the mainland of Greece, on which is scratched a primitive kind of writing. For many years it seemed impossible to make out even what language they were written in, but nearly all scholars are now agreed that it is an early form of Greek. They consist mainly of lists and record in astonishing detail certain aspects of the life of the times. From Cnossus in Crete come lists of the number of sheep in a particular area and the amount of wool they would yield in one year; from Pylos in south-west Greece we have a series of eighteen tablets recording the contributions to be made to the palace storehouse by various villages; others give information about the ownership of land or are lists of military equipment or slaves. They show that the citadels of Mycenaean Greece were the centres of elaborate bureaucracies and that they depended not only on military power but also on a vast army of clerks.

The Mycenaean civilisation flourished not only on the mainland of Greece but also on the Aegean islands, including Crete. It traded with Egypt and Syria and with Sicily and southern Italy and even, perhaps, with Britain.

14. *Linear* B *Tablet: a list of tripod cauldrons and other vessels from Pylos. The translation of the first line runs:* '2 *tripod cauldrons of Cretan workmanship of* ai-ke-u *type;* 1 *tripod cauldron with a single handle;* 1 *tripod cauldron of Cretan workmanship, burnt away at the legs, useless.*'

ɔ ke-re-si-jo we-ke a-pu ke-ka-u-me-no

i-pa me-wi-jo qe-to-ro-we POT 1

67

15. *Mycenae: the citadel from the south-west.*

Troy

Troy too was part of the Mycenaean world. Like the citadels of mainland Greece it was small, only about 550 yards in circumference. Unlike them, it contained at the time of its destruction not merely a palace and a few spacious houses but a large number of small, poorly-built ones, huddled together just inside the walls. Nearly all of them had storage jars hidden beneath the floor. It looks as if life outside the walls had become dangerous and that the local population had flocked into the city and was expecting repeated attack or even siege. When Troy was destroyed it was by a fire, which seems to have been started deliberately.

The collapse of Mycenaean Greece and the Dark Age

All this suggests that the legend of the siege of Troy may have some solid historical fact behind it. But scholars are undecided whether it was the Mycenaean Greeks who were responsible for its destruction. This is because at almost the same time as Troy was destroyed Mycenae itself and other leading states of mainland Greece were also destroyed. The reasons for their fall are not really known, but it is clear that there was widespread disturbance at this time in several parts of the eastern Mediterranean area, including Egypt and Syria, and among the Hittites of central Turkey. At

16. *Old Smyrna, shortly before 600* B.C.

such a time the Greeks may well not have been strong enough to mount a major overseas expedition.

The civilisation of Mycenaean Greece collapsed totally. A new branch of the Greek race, the Dorians, occupied much of Greece. They were illiterate and they lacked the technical skills in building and metal-work which the Mycenaeans had had. Very little evidence survives from the next four hundred years, and historians often refer to it as the Dark Age.

Greece around 800 BC

When the Dark Age ends around 800 there have been many changes. Iron has replaced bronze as the normal metal for cutting tools. The Greeks are now settled not only in the mainland and on the Aegean islands but also in the rich coastal valleys of western Turkey, particularly in the area the Greeks called Ionia. In the early part of the Dark Age most Greek states were ruled by kings, but by about 800 the usual form of organisation over most of the Greek world was the *polis*. This was an independent community, generally under aristocratic rule. It consisted of an urban centre, which was generally quite small – Old Smyrna, for instance, one of the most prosperous cities of Ionia, had a total population at the time of about two thousand – and the country surrounding it.

Writing and Colonisation

Between 800 and 700 the Greeks began to trade again with Syria and the eastern Mediterranean. The most important result of this renewed contact was that the Greeks took over and adapted to their own language the alphabet then used in the coastal cities of northern Syria. (This alphabet, in the form used by the Romans, is the one we use nowadays.) About 750 the Greeks started to expand into the western Mediterranean by colonising the coastal areas of Sicily and southern Italy.

Mycenaean Greece and the Greece which emerged from the Dark Age were very different. Which does Homer describe in the *Iliad* and *Odyssey*?

17. '*Lion Hunt*' *Dagger Blade, made in about 1500 B.C.; the blade is of bronze, inlaid with gold, silver and niello, and is about nine inches long.*

Iliad and Odyssey

Mycenaean features in Homer

When archaeologists began to excavate Mycenaean sites in the late nineteenth century, they were delighted to realise that their discoveries often fitted very closely with the picture given by Homer. For example, the metal used for weapons in the Mycenaean world was bronze, though iron took its place early in the Dark Age. Homer regularly speaks of bronze spears and swords.

Body shields

Again, in *Iliad* VI [117–18] we read that as Hector turned from the battle to go back to Troy 'the dark leather rim at the edge of his shield tapped against his ankles and the back of his neck'; while in *Iliad* VII [219] Ajax is said to carry a shield 'like a tower'; in fact, it is big enough for his brother, the archer Teucer, to hide beneath [*Iliad* VIII 266]. An illustration of these huge body shields can be seen on the famous 'Lion Hunt' dagger blade which Schliemann found at Mycenae. Shields of this pattern went out of use in Greece by 1100. This dagger blade is also a superb example of the technique of inlaying metals, which was forgotten at the end of the Mycenaean period but is referred to in the elaborate description of the shield which Hephaestus made for Achilles [*Iliad* XVIII].

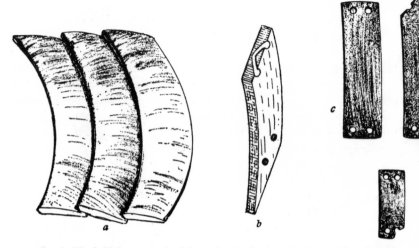

18.   *Boar's Tusk Helmet: on the left, a sketch showing the slivers of boar's tusk and the way they were fitted together; on the right, a drawing of two small ivory heads showing men wearing helmets of this type.*

Boar's Tusk Helmet

Sometimes the objects archaeologists found provided an explanation of passages in the poems which had not previously been understood. For example, in *Iliad* x

> Meriones gave Odysseus a bow, a quiver, and a sword, and set upon his head a helmet made of leather; inside, it was made of tightly interwoven thongs, while on the outside the flashing white tusks of boars had been skilfully arranged to run thickly this way and that; in between the two a layer of felt had been fitted. [*Iliad* x 260–5.]

Scholars had not been able to visualise such helmets until archaeologists discovered at a number of sites small slivers of boar's tusk, pierced at either end so that they could be attached to some backing, and some ivory figures of men wearing helmets of this type. It seems that these helmets were not made after about 1100.

Political Geography

If we look at the political geography of the poems and try to discover which states Homer considered the most important at the time of the Trojan War, we find that his opinions usually coincide with those of the archaeologists. In the Catalogue of the Greek Forces in *Iliad* II we read how many ships each Greek leader brought to Troy. The states which are the most powerful in the Catalogue – Mycenae, Argos, Sparta, and Pylos –

a

b

are just the ones archaeologists would choose as a result of their excavations. Moreover, Mycenae and Pylos were quite insignificant after the collapse of Mycenaean power. Again, Homer hardly mentions the Dorians or the Greek settlements in Ionia, which occurred, as we have seen, after the fall of Mycenaean Greece.

Schliemann decided to excavate at Troy and Mycenae because he believed that the *Iliad* and *Odyssey* were historically accurate. The sort of evidence mentioned above strengthened his belief. One of the main reasons why few people share it today is that Homer never mentions what modern scholars consider one of the most typical features of the Mycenaean world – the system of palace bureaucracy revealed by the Linear B tablets.

Post-Mycenaean features in Homer

Another reason is that Homer also mentions several objects and practices which are post-Mycenaean.

Temples
In *Iliad* VI (86–9) Helenus suggests that while he and Aeneas stay on the battlefield to resist the Greek advance, Hector should return to Troy and tell his mother to gather the old women together and lead them to the temple of Athena. This temple is clearly a separate building, but archaeologists believe that the earliest examples of such temples date from shortly before 800. In Mycenaean times a room in the palace was set aside for worship.

19. *Cauldron and Tripod, from Olympia, ninth century* B.C.

Tripods and Cauldrons

Among the gifts which Agamemnon offers to Achilles in the hope of persuading him to return to the fight are 'seven tripods, not yet touched by the fire . . . and twenty burnished cauldrons' [*Iliad* IX 122–3]. Although there must have been tripods and cauldrons in the Mycenaean world, it was in the Dark Age that they were treated as valuable possessions; they became in fact a common form of offering to the gods.

20. *Bronze Head of Griffin, from Samos, seventh century* B.C.; *the head was designed to stand on the rim of a cauldron such as that in Illustration 19.*

Colonisation

Again, in the *Odyssey* we read that

> Athena went to the city of the Phaeacians, who had formerly lived in Hyperia. . . . Godlike Nausithous led them away from there and settled them in Scheria. He drove a wall round the city, built houses, constructed temples of the gods, and divided out the land for cultivation. [*Odyssey* VI 2–10.]

Here Homer seems to be describing the way the Greeks set up a colony, and this is a process which started only around 750 BC.

The general picture

Above all, the general picture the poems give is of the post-Mycenaean world. The Greek legend spoke of Agamemnon as commander-in-chief of a huge alliance, but neither in the *Iliad* nor in the *Odyssey* does Homer seem aware of the complex organisation that would be necessary to control such an alliance on an overseas expedition. Agamemnon, Odysseus and their fellow-kings resemble, not the Mycenaean kings at the head of their tightly-controlled bureaucracies, but the primitive and illiterate warrior kings of early Dark Age Greece. Most of the other detailed pictures of social life are also post-Mycenaean.

Homer and history

Homer is not a historian, but a bard of the kind described in Chapter 2. The oral tradition in which he worked included references to objects from the Mycenaean period, remembered and passed down from bard to bard over a period of at least four hundred years. It also incorporated references to later objects and later patterns of behaviour at every stage from the fall of the Mycenaean world to Homer's own day. The members of his audience were not interested in matters of historical accuracy or consistency in the way we are. We should try to accept Homer as he was, appreciating his qualities as a poet and not worrying if he does not supply us with the historical information we should like to possess.

Homer and the Greeks

The Greeks regarded Homer as their greatest poet. They could even refer to him without confusion simply as 'the poet'. His influence on Greek life was colossal and can be seen in many fields.

Around 570–65 the Athenians and the inhabitants of the neighbouring state of Megara were fighting for possession of the island of Salamis. When their quarrel went to arbitration the Athenians put forward as evidence for their right to rule it a couple of lines from the Catalogue of the Greek Forces in *Iliad* II – 'Ajax brought twelve ships from Salamis and beached them next to the Athenians' [*Iliad* II 557–8]. This proved, they argued, that Athens and Salamis had been associated for a long time.

Vase-painters frequently took their subjects from the *Iliad* and *Odyssey*, and several of their works have been used as illustrations in this book. In their attitude to Homer they vary considerably. Some treat his narrative quite freely (10, 13), others approach an incident in a spirit almost of comedy (3), while others again are close in mood and detail to the Homeric original (4, 12).

In Chapter 4 we described Homer's attitude to the gods as anthropomorphic. This remained the typical Greek attitude thereafter, and several writers including the poet Xenophanes, who came from Ionia and lived towards the end of the sixth century, and the historian Herodotus, who was writing in the second half of the fifth century, claimed that Homer and a slightly later poet called Hesiod had been responsible for this, by inventing the characters and attributes of the gods. Xenophanes pointed out that these characters were hardly ideal: 'Homer and Hesiod attributed to the gods all the crimes of mankind – theft, adultery, and cheating one another' (*Fr.* 10D). The philosopher Plato also criticised Homer for making the gods no better than mortals.

APOTHEOSIS OF HOMER.
INSCRIBED WITH NAME OF SCULPTOR ARCHELAOS OF PRIENE.
BOVILLÆ, ON THE APPIAN WAY, FORMERLY IN THE COLONNA PALACE, ROME.

21. *The Apotheosis of Homer. The Greeks' belief that Homer was their greatest poet is demonstrated by this relief sculpture dating from the second century* B.C. *It shows Homer (seated in the bottom row) being crowned by Time and the World; he is saluted by figures representing Poetry, Tragedy and Comedy, while in the upper rows are gods and muses.*

But it was in the field of education and morals that the influence of Homer was greatest. Plato claimed that Homer had been the 'educator of Greece', and there was hardly any exaggeration in the claim. Once Greek children had learned their letters, their first continuous reading consisted of lines from the *Odyssey*. The *Iliad* and *Odyssey* were always the books most used in Greek schools, and we know of Greeks who could recite them both by heart. Certainly all educated Greeks could quote freely from them from memory.

Moreover, this educational process helped to keep alive the ideal of the Homeric hero. It was aristocratic in outlook, but its influence remained very powerful even in such democratic states as fifth century Athens. This can be seen very clearly in the career of the politician Alcibiades. During the course of his life he was first an Athenian democrat and military leader, then deserted to assist the Spartans against his own city, was next involved in intrigues to bring down the democracy at Athens in favour of an oligarchy, and finally changed sides again to become leader of the democracy he had twice betrayed. His only aim was success, his only principle 'always to be best and excel other men' [*Iliad* XI 784].

Alexander the Great is said to have carried a copy of the *Iliad* with him wherever he went. Almost the first thing he did when he landed in Turkey, at the start of the campaigns which were to destroy the Persian Empire and to spread Greek civilisation to the frontiers of India, was to visit Troy. He sacrificed to the heroes who were buried there, and especially to Achilles. When someone suggested that he might like to see the harp of Paris, which was preserved there, he refused but added that he would have been glad to see the harp which Achilles used when he sang of the exploits of heroes.

Indexes

Index A gives an expanded list of the topics covered in each chapter. The first page references are to the main treatment of the topic within that chapter; other references follow this.

Index B is a list of proper names.